Joseph Bellamy

Theron, Paulinus and Aspasio

Letters and dialogues upon the nature of love to God

Joseph Bellamy

Theron, Paulinus and Aspasio
Letters and dialogues upon the nature of love to God

ISBN/EAN: 9783337216917

Printed in Europe, USA, Canada, Australia, Japan

Cover: Foto ©Lupo / pixelio.de

More available books at **www.hansebooks.com**

Theron, Paulinus, and Aspasio.

OR,

LETTERS & DIALOGUES

UPON THE NATURE OF

Love to God, Faith in Christ, Assurance

OF A

Title to Eternal Life,

CONTAINING

SOME REMARKS ON THE SENTIMENTS

OF THE

Reverend Messieurs Hervey and Marshal,

ON THESE SUBJECTS.

Published at the REQUEST of MANY.

By JOSEPH BELLAMY, A. M.

Minister of the Gospel, at Bethlem, in New-England.

"*Amidst all the darkness and uncertainty, which evidently run
through the Writings of the best of Men, this is our unspeakable happiness, that we have a more sure Word of Prophecy;
to which we do well to take heed.—As for Offence; that
cannot be given, and ought not to be taken, when all we
advance is strictly conformable to the unerring rule of Truth.
I have nothing to do with the persons of Men, but with the
Truths of the Gospel. Ouranius, though eminently devout,
may be mistaken.*" HERVEY.

WASHINGTON:

PRINTED BY JOHN COLERICK, AND MAY BE
HAD OF ALL THE STORE-KEEPERS.

1798.

Letters and Dialogues, &c.

LETTER I.

THERON TO ASPASIO.

New-England, Dec. 15, 1758.

DEAR ASPASIO,

NEWS from your Theron, now in this remote corner of the Earth, you will eagerly expect by every ship that sails from these parts.—But what shall I write, O my friend!—No pleasant walks, no beautiful gardens, no romantic mounts, my dear Aspasio, nor any other theme to entertain and to amuse must you expect from me! Alas, I have been deceived! My hopes, once high raised, are, I think, entirely gone. *As the rush without mire, and the flag without water; so the hypocrite's hope shall perish.* (1)

As I was walking in my garden, soon after our visit to Philenor, (2) (which was, as I remember, about the middle of harvest A. D. 1754,) musing on all your agreeable conversation, your fervent zeal, and how you urged me to believe:—To believe what? said I, to myself.—To believe that Christ died for ME.—How, for ME? thought I.—Aspasio knows, I believe that Christ died for sinners.—Yes, but he would have me apply that to my own soul; and believe Christ died for me.—Aspasio knows, I believe

---

(1) *Job* viii. 11, 13. See Mr. Hervey's Dialogues, Vol. III. p. 313. edit. I.—N. B. The first *edition of Mr. Herv. Dial. is referred to in this letter: as Theron is supposed soon after the conversation at Philenor's, to have experienced what follows.*

(2) Mr. Hervey's Dialogues, vol. III. p. 262.

that Christ died; that whosoever, according to the true sense of the Gospel, believes in him, should not perish, but have everlasting life. Is this believing in him?—Is this justifying saving Faith?—To believe I am ONE that he died for—one for whom he intended to procure pardon, reconciliation with God and eternal life?—Yes, this, this is Faith. "A real persuasion that the blessed Jesus has shed his blood for me, and fulfilled all righteousness in my stead, that through this great atonement and glorious obedience, he has purchased, even for my sinful soul, sanctifying grace, and all spiritual blessings."(1) To believe it was for ME, just as if I had been mentioned by NAME: even just as my Tenant believed me, when, in his last sickness, I sent a message, assuring him, I had cancelled the bond, and forgiven his debt. (2) And just as David believed the kingdom of Israel should be his own, on the express promise of Almighty God. (3) And just as I believed my lands to be my own, by the deeds of conveyance. (4) In a word, Aspasio would have me go to God, and say, "Pardon is mine, grace is mine, Christ and all his spiritual blessings are mine;" not because I am conscious of sanctifying operations in my own breast, but because I am conscious I am a sinner. All these blessings being consigned over to me as such, in the everlasting Gospel; with a clearness unquestionable as the truth, with a certainty inviolable as the oath of God. (5) No clogging qualifications insisted on: only believe, and all is mine. (6) I longed to know that Christ was mine. (7)

  And could I see my title clear,
  To mansions in the skies,
  I'd bid farewell to every tear
  And wipe my weeping eyes.

But how can I see! how can I believe! Oh my unbelieving heart! what shall I do?—"Cry to God for help," says my Aspasio. "Seek the blessed spirit to testify, that God has given me eternal life; and this life is in his Son. And to witness with my spirit, that I am a child of God (8).

Thus, as I walked, I mused—my heart was full—I stopped—with eyes lift up to Heaven, and said,—I believe,

(1) *Mr. Her. Dial. vol.* III. *p.* 278.   (2) *Ibid p.* 279.
(3) *P.* 309.   (4) *P.* 312.   (5) *P.* 280, 313.   (6) *P.* 275.
(7) *P.* 253, 254.   (8) *P.* 316.

Lord, help my unbelief.—I thought of Calvary.—I heard the foundings of his bowels, and of his mercies towards me. *O thou of little Faith! wherefore dost thou doubt?* (1) Wherefore dost thou doubt of my love to thee, for whom I have shed my blood?

I believed, I was ravished; I was full of love, joy and gratitude: and with eyes again lift up to Heaven, I said, "Glory be to the Holy Ghost for testifying of Christ in my heart, and appropriating this great salvation to my soul." (2) And thus I continued rejoicing for several days, and thought I should never doubt again.

But, oh, alas! the scene soon changed. I gradually lost a sense of my great danger, and great deliverance; as the Israelites, who sang God's praise, but soon forgat his works: or like the stony-ground hearers, who heard the Word with joy, endured for a while, and fell away. Or rather like the thorny-ground: for, as about this time I removed into New-England, the cares of the world came in upon me, and choaked the Word, and I brought forth no fruit: rather I lost all disposition to pray or praise, and my devotions degenerated into mere formality.

And now unbelief, as I then called it, began to work. "Surely all is mere delusion," thought I. But, again, I said, "This is my infirmity." And those words of Scripture were some comfort to me, *O thou of little Faith, wherefore dost thou doubt?—Who against Hope believed in Hope.—Who walk in darkness and see no light, let them trust in the Lord, and stay themselves on their God.—Why art thou cast down, O my Soul, hope thou in God?* (3) And I watched and prayed, and strove against my unbelieving thoughts. (4)

From this time forward, having no clear marks or signs of Grace for my comfort, nor any new manifestations of the love of God to my Soul, I began, as you had directed in such a case, to *live by Faith*. I used every day to go to God, and say, "Pardon is mine, grace is mine, Christ and all his spiritual blessings are mine." And thus, unconscious of any sanctifying operations in my own breast, I lived wholly by Faith: by Faith, as I thought, on the promise and oath of the unchangeable JEHOVAH. (5) And thus I

(1) *Herv. Dial. p.* 276, 277.   (2) *Vol.* I. *p.* 156.   (3) *P.* 289.   (4) *P.* 308, 309.   (5) *P.* 313, 314.

continued many months, generally pretty easy; although sometimes troubled with doubts and fears.

But above a year ago, as I was reading my bible, in the 13th chapter of St. Matthew's Gospel, I found the parable of the Sower; which reached my case, and greatly gained the attention of my heart. Here I saw the various sorts of hearers, the different kinds of Christians described; and perceived that none are esteemed good men by our blessed Saviour, but those who, like the good ground, *bring forth fruit*. This startled me, this gave my faith a shock, I never could get over!

However, not knowing but that I mistook the meaning of that parable, I resolved to search the Scriptures, to see if it were really the character of all true believers, to *bring forth fruit*, i.e. as I understood it, to be holy in heart and life. I began with the Gospel of St. Matthew, and read the New-Testament through, and made a collection of many texts of Scripture, which I wrote down and commented upon. I will give you a specimen from my Diary.

"*Nov.* 20, 1757, I retired as usual to read the holy Scriptures, by which I am to be judged at the last day.—I began to read Christ's Sermon on the Mount: *Blessed are the poor in spirit; Blessed are they that mourn; Blessed are the meek;—the pure of heart,* &c. But alas, O my Soul! I am not conscious of these good qualifications: are there not, nevertheless, blessings laid up for me?——I read on to chapter vii. 19, 27. *Every tree that bringeth not forth good fruit, is hewn down and cast into the fire: By their fruits ye shall know them: Not every one that saith unto me, Lord, Lord, shall enter into the kingdom of Heaven, but he that doeth the will of my Father which is in Heaven.* This, this, O my Soul, reaches my very case! this is my character! and this my doom! The following verses condemn me too: I am the man that has *built his house upon the sand.*" Thus far my Diary.

But how discouraging soever all this appeared, yet still I maintained some secret thoughts, that I was only a backslider, and should see things clearer after a while. Besides, to give up my hopes, and look upon myself a poor Christless sinner, after I had so long settled down in quiet, was like death to my spirits;—It opened a most frightful prospect before me.—If not converted now, most probably I never shall be! I had as good live on in pleasing delusion, as sink down into despair!

And besides, I remembered you had said, "This method of seeking peace and assurance," by signs of Grace, "I fear, will embarrass the simple minded, and cherish rather than suppress the fluctuations of doubt; for let the marks be what you please, they are all a feeble and precarious evidence." And I wished I could boldly say, as once I did, "Pardon is mine, grace is mine, Christ and all his spiritual blessings are mine; however unconscious of sanctifying operations in my own breast. (1) But our blessed Saviour's words struck terror through my soul: *He that heareth these words of mine and doth them not, is like a foolish man, that built his house upon the sand.*

About this time I was, by a religious Person well acquainted with my case, directed to Mr. Shepherd " on the Parable of the Ten Virgins;" Mr. Edwards " on Religious Affections, Mr. Bainard's Life," and some other books of the same stamp; "which, (said he) are esteemed by pious people in New-England, as the best of books on experimental religion." I obtained the books, I read them, they condemned not only my present state, but all my notions of religion: and represented true religion to consist in something essentially different, of which I had never had the least experience: which instead of affording comfort and hope to my dejected mind, did but confirm my former doubts and fears. What now to do, I could not tell—Here three thousand miles from my dear Aspasio, I cannot see his face, nor have his aid.—I must find out another spiritual guide—I heard of one Paulinus, a clergyman, a noted friend to vital piety, a tender faithful guide to bewildered souls; but not in my Aspasio's scheme. My conscience said, " Go see the man, and act an honest part; tell him all your case, be willing to know the truth." My heart replied, " I cannot go! I cannot go!" But as a serious, solemn sense of the eternal world was now daily growing in my heart, I was soon brought to a better mind; particularly in the evening of *December* 8, 1758. As I was alone for secret prayer, I had such a sense of eternity, a boundless eternity, and such a view of the dreadfulness of eternal damnation—the amazement and horror of self-deceived hypocrites, opening their eyes in eternal woe, who once refused to see,

(1) *Herv. Dial.* p. 313.

while there was hope, but now muſt ſee when all hope is for ever gone; that I ſhuddered, and was ready even to cry out with anguiſh at the terrifying thought of this being at laſt my dreadful lot! Whereupon, reſolving to be honeſt at all adventures, I determined on a viſit the next Monday evening.—I went, I went again and again; and knowing my dear Aſpaſio would be glad to hear what paſſed, I wrote, down the ſubſtance from time to time, which I now ſend encloſed, in the form of *Three Dialogues;* which, when you have read, I am ſure you will pity my caſe.—And, O my Aſpaſio, ceaſe not to pray for

Your diſconſolate
THERON.

P. S. I expect no opportunity to write you again till early next Spring; when you may look to hear further from your Theron, if on this ſide eternal burnings.—God only knows how that will be. Adieu, my dear Aſpaſio.

DIALOGUE I.

ON Monday evening *(Decem.* 11.*)* I had the happineſs to find Paulinus at home, alone in his ſtudy; he received me with all the politeneſs of a Gentleman, and with all the undiſſembled goodneſs of a Chriſtian. After enquiring into the ſtate of Religion in Great-Britain, when I came from thence; perceiving by what was ſaid, my acquaintance with Aſpaſio, he made ſome enquiries after him, and his ſentiments of Religion, and about a book he has lately ſo ſtrongly recommended. (1) Which gave me

---

(1) Mr. *Marſhal's Goſpel-Myſtery of Sanctification;*—*" which I ſhall not (ſays Mr. Hervey) recommend in the ſtile of a critic, or like a reader of taſte, but with all the ſimplicity of the weakeſt Chriſtian; I mean from my own experience.*

an opportunity, without letting him into the state of my Soul, a thing I was loth to do, to bring upon the board the topics I designed. Wherefore, I began——

Theron. Sir, may I know your sentiments relative to some points in these books?

Paulinus. I am willing you should know my sentiments on any of the doctrines of Religion; but should chuse to say nothing of the sentiments of any particular author by name.

Ther. I am sensible this is not so desirable, nor should I ask it, but that I am not a little embarrassed between the scheme of Religion advanced in President Edwards's Treatise on Religious Affections, and this advanced in these books: And I want to know, what may be said in answer to the particular arguments of these Divines. And I shall consider all you say, how plain soever: for I desire you to use the greatest freedom, not in a personal light, as designed to reflect at all on these authors; but only as designed to give instruction to me. And if you could particularly answer several things I find in them, it would give me much more satisfaction, than to hear your opinion in general.—Besides you know, what authors publish to the world, they voluntarily submit to the examination of all. And if the good of mankind, which all authors profess to seek, calls for a particular examination of any of their writings, they cannot consistently be displeased, if they are used with candor. These authors themselves have taken the greatest freedom to speak of the sentiments of Divines, ancient and modern. And I know my dear Aspasio would be perfectly pleased to hear you, with the utmost freedom, make all your remarks and observations on his piece; for he is one

---

It has been made one of the most useful books to my own soul; I scarce ever fail to receive spiritual consolation and strength from the perusal of it. And was I to be banished into some desolate Island, possessed only of two books besides my bible, this should be one of the two, and perhaps the first that I would choose." See Mr. Hervey's Dialogues, edit. 3. vol. III. p. 336.

N. B. *This 3d edition of Mr. Hervey's Dial. is referred to in what follows. And the 6th edition of Mr. Marshal.——* D. *shall stand for Mr. Hervey's Dialogues, vol.* III.——M. *shall stand for Mr. Marshal's Gospel-Mystery,* &c. *As both these books contain one complete system, so both shall be considered together.*

of the most candid, generous, good-natured gentlemen I ever saw: Pray, Sir, therefore make no excuses, nor be at all upon the reserve.

Paul. What particular points, Sir, do you refer to?

Ther. The nature of LOVE TO GOD, of JUSTIFYING FAITH, and of ASSURANCE.—To begin with Love to God. I desire to know what is the primary and chief motive, which ought to induce me to love God. A view of the ineffable glories of the Deity, as he has manifested himself in his word and in his works? Or a belief of his love to me in particular?

Paul. Before we enquire into the original grounds of love to God, pray tell me, What in God are we to love? and how are we to love him?

Ther. "The Lord is not at all loved with that love that is due to him as Lord of all, if he be not loved with all our heart and spirit, and might. And we are to love every thing in him, his Justice, Holiness, sovereign Authority, all-seeing Eye, and all his Decrees, Commands, Judgments, and all his doings." (1)

Paul. Who are under obligations thus to love God? Saints, or Sinners? Christians, or Heathens? Some, or all of mankind.

Ther. All mankind. Even the Heathen, who are without any written law or supernatural revelation, are obliged by the light of Nature to love God with all their hearts; and that under the penalty of God's everlasting wrath. (2)

Paul. If all mankind, even the Heathen world not excepted, are thus under infinite obligations to love God with all their hearts, and to *glorify God as God*, (to use the Apostle's expression, Rom. i. 21.) it must needs be that there is a ground and reason of love to God antecedent to a consideration of his being our reconciled Father and Friend in Jesus Christ. For the Heathen, millions of them, never heard of Jesus Christ. And there are great multitudes in the Christian world, who live and die without an interest in God's fatherly love in Christ. And yet you say, all these are under such obligations to love God with all their hearts, that they will deserve his eternal wrath for the least neglect. And indeed the holy Scriptures most expressly assert the same thing, Rom. i. 18—21. Gal. iii. 10.

(1) M. *p.* 2.   (2) M. *p.* 4, 5.

Ther. But, Sir, is it not impossible (1) we should love God before we see that he is our reconciled Father and Friend in Jesus Christ? We must know that our sins are forgiven, and be well persuaded that God is reconciled to us, before we can love him. (2)

Paul. God never manifests himself as a reconciled God and Father, to any of the children of men, until they are first reconciled to him, and love him. John xiv. 21. Acts iii. 19. Their first love to God, therefore, must of necessity begin on some other foundation, from some other inducement; or they never can begin to love him at all.

Ther. But what is there in God, that can induce us to love him, unless we first know that he loves us? I appeal to the experience of all true Saints, as inconsistent with your supposition. (3)

Paul. This is the language of God's law, *Thou shalt love the Lord thy God with all thy heart.* Pray, what reasons and grounds are there for this law? Answer my question first, and then I will answer your's. Tell me the grounds and reasons of this law, and I will tell you what there is to induce us to love God before we know that he loves us.

Ther. The law teaches us, first to believe that God is our GOD, our reconciled Father and Friend: *Thou shalt love the Lord* THY GOD. (4)

Paul. God is our GOD, the God of the whole human race, as he is our Creator, our Preserver, our rightful Lord and Sovereign, who has an entire and absolute authority

---

(1) Should a lying fellow bring tidings to an impenitent prisoner justly condemned to die for murder, assuring him of a pardon from his judge; the deluded murderer might be full of love to his judge, and greatly extol his justice, as well as goodness, and pour out floods of tears: But on discerning his mistake, he would soon return to his former temper. God's nature and law are just the same, before he forgives us, as after; and as worthy to be loved. But it is easier for an impenitent sinner to commend God's law, in a firm belief he is delivered from the curse. than to love it as being in its own nature holy, just, and good. Satan knows, it is no evidence of Uprightness in God's account, that a man is very religious; if all his Religion arises merely from selfish considerations. Job i. 8, 9, 10, 11.

(2) M. *p.* 21, 25.   (3) M. *p.* 25.   (4) M. *p.* 28.

over us: But he is not a reconciled Father and Friend to all the human race. Rather *the whole world lieth in wickedness*, 1 John v. 19. And the greatest part of mankind are under the divine wrath. John iii. 36. And God is *angry with them every day; his soul hates them, and he is whetting his sword for their destruction, if they repent not.* Psalm vii. 11, 12, and xi. 5. And yet even while in such a state, you grant, they are under infinite obligations to love God with all their hearts; and that the least defect exposes them to eternal damnation. Nor have you granted any more than St. Paul expressly asserts, Gal. iii. 10.—Now, pray, tell me, is this a reasonable law?

Ther. I grant, this law is holy, just and good. (1)

Paul. But then it will follow, that there are reasons and grounds why God should be thus loved, antecedent to a consideration of his being our reconciled Father and Friend. Reasons and grounds which are sufficient; which really oblige us in point of duty: and therefore ought to influence us in practice. And if we are not influenced by them, we are to blame. Yea, so much to blame, you say, as to deserve God's eternal wrath.

Ther. It is certain, that all the perfection, goodness and excellency of the divine nature, cannot render God an amiable object to us, unless we know that he loves us, and is our reconciled Father and Friend. (2)

Paul. The first question is not, whether unregenerate sinners, while dead in sin, and enemies to God, do actually love God: but whether they ought not to love him. Whether the perfection, goodness and excellency of the divine nature is not a proper inducement, which renders it reasonable and fit: Yea, which obliges; nay, infinitely obliges them to love God. I think you must grant this; for how else can the law be holy, just and good?

Ther. If I should grant that the perfection, goodness and excellency of the divine nature, does render it fit and reasonable that we should love God with all our hearts; yet it is impossible we should love him, except first we know he loves us. (3)

Paul. If God is really a Being infinitely amiable in himself, and if it is fit and reasonable we should love him for the perfection, goodness and excellency of his nature, then

(1) M. *p.* 4. (2) M. *p.* 25. (3) M. *p.* iv. 25.

there is, yea, there can be no difficulty in the way of the practice of this duty, but what lies in the badness of our hearts; and so, what we are to blame for. And therefore were our hearts right, we should love him for his own loveliness, (1) and feel disposed to glorify God, AS GOD; as the very Heathen ought to do, who never heard of his designs of mercy by Jesus Christ. Nay, all the Heathen world are at this day, and ever have been entirely without excuse, in not being thus affected towards the infinitely glorious God that made them: Yea, they are, for this, infinitely to blame; so as to deserve eternal wrath. And this is St. Paul's doctrine, Rom. i. 18, 21. Nay, this doctrine is fundamental to St. Paul's whole scheme of Religion.— Overthrow this, and you will overthrow his whole scheme. For it is in this view, that he pronounces Jew and Gentile, even the whole world, to stand guilty before God, with their mouths stopt, without one excuse to make for themselves, though doomed to eternal destruction for not loving God with all their hearts. And so holy, just and good does he esteem this law to be, as that it was needful the Son of God should be set forth to be a propitiation, to declare God's righteousness, that HE MIGHT BE JUST, and not go counter to all good rules of government in pardoning and saving true penitents. Rom. iii. 9, 26.

Ther. The Heathen were liable to destruction for their idolatries, and gross immoralities.

Paul. Yes, and also for their not glorifying God AS GOD. *The wrath of God,* says the Apostle, *is revealed from Heaven against* ALL *ungodliness:* against the least degree of disrespect towards the infinitely glorious Majesty of Hea-

---

(1) *If our hearts were right,* i. e. *were as they ought to be, were as the law requires them to be, we should love God for his own loveliness: But in regeneration our hearts begin to be right; therefore, then, even at that instant, we begin to love God for his own loveliness. For at that very instant when* the vail is taken from our hearts, we all with open face, beheld as in a glass, the glory of the Lord, 2 *Cor.* iii. 18. *Even the law as a ministration of death and condemnation appears glorious, ver.* 7. 9.———*But every man is to blame, that his heart is not right.* Theron *pleads impossibility.* St. Paul, *however declares this kind of impossibility to be no excuse, Rom. i.* 20, 21.

ven. The least defect of love towards God, exposes them to eternal destruction. This was the Apostle's constant doctrine, and a chief foundation of his whole scheme of principles. Gal. iii. 10. Rom. i. 18, and iii. 20.

Ther. But the Gentiles had not so much as heard of the way of salvation by Christ; and must therefore, if their consciences were awakened, be in fearful expectation of eternal wrath. But surely it must be absolutely impossible we should love God, if we view him, as disposed to punish us in Hell for ever. Yea, "if I look on God as contrary to me, as one that hates me and will damn me, my own innate self-love will breed hatred and heart-risings against him in spight of my heart." (1)

Paul. That is, the divine law is so intolerably cruel, that unless it is entirely set aside as to us, we can never be pacified towards our maker. We are in arms, in open rebellion, so virulent that we are full of " hatred and heart-risings," in spite of all restraints. And we proclaim in the sight of Heaven, our cause is so just, that we can never lay down our arms, fall at the foot of our sovereign and justify his law; nay we can never have one good thought of him, till first he set aside his law, remove the curse, and grant us Heaven upon our demands. Upon this condition we will forgive our Lawgiver for what is past, and be at peace for the future. On this foot we will lay down our arms, and be reconciled. Our first work, therefore is, to believe that God doth give Christ and his salvation to us, and is become our reconciled Father and Friend. And this belief is to lay the foundation of all our Religion. But, O my dear Theron, such a Faith, growing up out of such an unhumbled, unsubdued heart as this, and a Religion arising from such a root, is all delusion, if there be any such thing in nature as delusion. (2)

Besides, tell me, my Theron, do you verily believe, that God's disposition to punish sin, according to his holy Law,

(1) M. *p.* 140.
(2) *How righteous is it, in the holy Sovereign of the world, to suffer such a proud, self-righteous Sinner, so ready to quarrel for a pardon, to be deluded with a false persuasion that he is pardoned! As he takes Satan's side against God and his Laws; so God may justly leave him in Satan's power,* 2 Thess. ii. 10, 11, 12.

is a hateful difpofition? And do you verily believe, that God is an odious Being on this account? Or do you allow yourfelf to hate God, for that, for which he appears infinitely amiable in the eyes of all the Heavenly world? Rev. xix. 1, 6. Or is your heart a carnal, unregenerate heart, under the full power of enmity againſt God and his Law? Rom. viii. 7. It is certain, what you ſay can never be juſtified. For if we have given God juſt cauſe to hate and puniſh us, by our wickedneſs, he is not the leſs lovely for being diſpoſed to do ſo, except he is the leſs lovely for being holy and juſt; that is, the leſs lovely, for that, in which his lovelineſs in a great meaſure confiſts.

You acknowledge the Law is *holy*, *juſt* and *good*, even as to the Heathen world, who never heard of a Saviour. Therefore, it is not the Grace of the Goſpel, that makes the Law good. The Law is older than the Goſpel, and was *holy*, *juſt* and *good*, before the Goſpel had a being.— Yea, the Law had been for ever good, if Chriſt had never died. We were not the injured, abuſed party: Chriſt did not die to make ſatisfaction to us, pacify our angry minds, and allay our "hatred and heart-riſings." The Grace of the Goſpel is not granted to counterbalance the rigour of the Law, and to render God's plan of government juſtifiable; and ſo to ſweeten the imbittered minds of God's enemies. God the Father, was not a tyrant, nor did his Son die a ſacrifice to tyranny, to reſcue his injured ſubjects from the ſeverities of a cruel Law. Nay, if the Law in all its rigour had not been *holy*, *juſt* and *good*, antecedent to the gift of Chriſt; there had been no need God ſhould ever give his Son to die, to anſwer its demands. It ought to have been repealed on Adam's fall, if too ſevere for an apoſtate race; and not honoured by the obedience and death of God's own Son. If this Law, as binding on a fallen world, is not, in itſelf, *holy*, *juſt* and *good*, glorious and amiable; the Goſpel of Chriſt is all deluſion. For it is impoſſible the Son of God ſhould die to anſwer the demands of an unrighteous Law. It was wrong he ſhould bear a curſe in our ſtead, which we ourſelves did not deſerve. Such an appointment would have been inconſiſtent with all the Divine perfections. If we view the Law as too severe, we must view the Gospel as not of God; if we will be consistent with ourselves. (1)

Therefore, you and I must approve the Law as holy, just and good, glorious and amiable, with application to ourselves, before we can with all our hearts believe the Gospel to be true. And therefore, not a belief of God's love to us, but a view of the infinite loveliness of the Divine Nature, must reconcile us to the Divine Law.—-Nor does this reasoning attempt to prove an impossibilty; but rather it demonstrates the absolute necessity of regeneration, as antecedent to the first act of Faith; a doctrine your

---

(1) *In Mr. Hervey's* ix. *Dialogue, Vol. II. p.* 16. *edit.* 1*st*. *Aspasio having cited the words of the Apostle, to prove his point :* As many as are of the works of the Law, are under the curse. *Gal. iii.* 10. *Theron objects, and Aspasio answers as follows.*

" Theron. *Under the curse! becuse our attempts to obey, though faithfully exerted, are attended with defects! Is not this unreasonable and shocking? Unreasonable that the God of Justice should establish a Law of such consummate perfection, as no child of Adam can, even with his utmost assiduity and care, fulfil! Shocking, that the God of Mercy should thunder out so severe a denunciation, on the least inadvertent breach, on every unavoidable failure!—This exceeds the relentless rigour of Draco, or the tyrannical impositions of the Egyptian task-masters. Draco is said to have written his laws in blood. Yet he never enacted such institutions, as were absolutely too strict and difficult to be observed. And though the Egyptian task-masters insisted upon the full tale of bricks without allowing the necessary proportion of straw, yet the punishment they inflicted, was incomparably less than everlasting destruction.*"

" Aspasio. *Had God Almighty's design in delivering his Law to fallen mankind, been to propound the means of their justification; your argument would have been valid, and your inference undeniable. But the Supreme legislator had a very different, a far more mysterious end.*" *That is, he designed the Law to be our schoolmaster, to bring us to Christ. As Aspasio goes on to shew, p.* 18, 19, 20—*without once thinking, that if the Law, antecedent to a consideration of the interposition and death of Christ, was a cruel Law, like that which the Egyptian task-masters urged, it ought to have been repealed.* It

author does not believe: (1) And yet a doctrine plainly taught in Scripture. Joh. 1, 12, 13.

Ther. Whatever we may do in speculation, when at ease; it is impossible, under a lively sense of the dreadfulness of eternal damnation, that we should, with application to ourselves, approve in our very hearts, the Law in all its rigour, as *holy, just* and *good,* as being really amiable and glorious in itself, till we know we are delivered from its Curse.

Paul. If the Law, in all it rigour, is not holy, just and good, glorious and amiable, before we are delivered from its curse, 'tis a pity the beloved Son of God was obliged to die to answer its demands. 'Tis a pity that a bad, a hateful Law should be so infinitely honoured in the sight of the whole intelligent system.—'Tis a pity God ever made it—a greater pity he suffered it to stand unrepealed. But the greatest pity of all that he gave his Son, his only begotten and well beloved Son, worshipped by all the hosts above, to die upon the shameful, painful Cross, to answer its demands. The Gospel opens a sad and gloomy scene

was a dishonour to God to make it, and a greater dishonour still to appoint his Son to answer its demands. Nor is a cruel Law fit to be a schoolmaster in God's world: or suited to teach us any thing, but to have hard thoughts of God. And yet Aspasio goes on to say (page 21) " *Rather than the Divine Law should lose its honours, Sodom and Gomorrah were laid in ashes; the ancient world was destroyed with a deluge; the present frame of Nature are destined to the flames, and all its unholy inhabitants must be doomed to Hell. Nay, rather than that the least tittle should pass unaccomplished, its curse has been executed on God's own Son, and all its injunctions have been fulfilled in the person of Jesus Christ.*" *Very true, but does not all this demonstrate, that the Law was not too severe and strict but perfectly* holy, just *and* good? —A glorious Law. 2 Cor. iii. 7. *And that previous to the consideration of the Grace of the Gospel. Had the Law been in itself bad, the death of Christ could not have made it good. Therefore, it was not* " *God's design,*" *that the Law should be our schoolmaster, that made the Law good: But it was in itself* holy, just *and* good; *and therefore, it was fit to be our schoolmaster.*

(1) M. p. 135.

to all the inhabitants of Heaven, if the Law is not a glorious Law. You may, O my Theron, be ravished to think Christ died for you, let the Law be good or bad; but you can never acquiesce in the Gospel way of life by the blood of Christ, as honourable to God, till the Law first appears glorious in your eyes: but rather (forgive me, my friend) I say, you will rather feel the heart of an infidel in your breast. You may be ravished to think Christ died for you; although you conceive of God the Father, as acting the part (Heaven forbid the blasphemy) I say, as acting the part of a tyrant in the whole affair. But then, who can be so stupid, as to believe the Son of God died a sacrifice to tyranny? "If you are safe, you care not how." Is this your heart? If so, you are quite an infidel.—Indeed, this is the heart of every natural man; and it is equally true, that every natural man is under the reigning power of infidelity. *No man can say, that Jesus is the Lord, but by the Holy Ghost.* 1 Cor. xii. 3. *Whosoever believeth that Jesus is the Christ, is born of God.* 1 Joh. v. 1. See also Rom. x. 9. 1 Joh. iv. 15. (1)

(1) *The external Evidences of Christianity may induce men to such a belief of the Gospel, as that they dare not renounce it, though they do not like it; but will not give a heart-satisfying conviction of its truth; so long as it seems to contain a system of doctrines inconsistent with the moral perfections of God. But at first sight, it appears inconsistent with the moral perfections of God, to give his Son to die in our stead, to answer the demands of a Law in its own nature too severe. So long, therefore, as the Law appears in this light, no man can heartily believe the report of the Gospel, Gal. iii.* 10, 13.—*And this is one reason, that all unregenerate men, who in Scripture are considered as enemies to God's Law (Rom. viii.* 7, 9.) *are represented as not believing the Gospel. (*1 John, v. 1, &c. &c.) *And this shews, how our unbelief of the Gospel arises from our enmity against God and his Law (John vii.* 17, *and viii.* 47.) *and so is truly criminal. (John iii.* 18, 19, 20, 21.—*And this accounts for the fearful apprehensions of eternal destruction so common to awakened Sinners, who begin to see their state by Law, but as yet do not approve the Law as holy, just and good. It is not strange their fears run so high, when they do not believe the Gospel to be true.—And this accounts for the aptness of awakened Sinners to catch hold of false hopes, and build on*

Wherefore, the awakened Sinner, under a lively senfe of the dreadfulnefs of eternal damnation, with particular application to himfelf, muft (through the regenerating influences of the holy Spirit) be brought to approve the law, in all its rigour, as *holy, juft* and *good,* as being really amiable and glorious in itfelf, before he can fo much as believe (in Scripture-fenfe) the Gofpel to be true. Till this, every man has the heart of an Infidel. Yea, till this, every man is as much of an enemy to the Gofpel (rightly underftood) as to the Law.

Here, my dear Theron, here lies the great difficulty of embracing Chriftianity. This fets the world againft it. Their hearts hate it, and their wits and pens are in a manner conftantly employed to banifh it from the face of the Earth. All the chief errors in Chriftendom grow up from a fecret hatred of God's holy Law. But all their elaborate volumes are confuted with this fingle fentence : *Chrift loved the*

falfe foundations: as they are blind to the only true way of efcape by Jefus Chrift. And this fhews how prepofterous it is, to think to perfuade Sinners to come to Chrift, and truft in him, before firft they approve the law by which they ftand condemned. They may be deluded by falfe fuggeftions and falfe joys; but they will never believe the Gofpel to be true with all their hearts, till firft they approve the law. Regeneration muft be before Faith. (John i. 12, 13.) As to the unthinking multitude, who believe any thing they know not why; they may believe the Gofpel juft as the Mahometans believe their Alcoran, merely becaufe their fathers believed it before them. But no thinking confiderate man, who has a right doctrinal underftanding of the Gofpel-plan, can ever believe it with all his heart, or cordially acquiefce in this way of life; till by feeing the glory of the God of Glory, he approves the Law as holy, juft and good; *and fo is prepared to fee the wifdom of God in the death of his Son.——See Mr. Edwards on the Affections,* p. 182, 199, *on the nature of Faith.——See, alfo, Mr. Edwards on the Freedom of the Will; in which all the objections of the Arminians againft the divine Law, as requiring more of us than we can do, are fapped at the foundation, fee page* 159, 177. *See alfo the Author's True Religion delineated, wherein his fentiments relative to the nature of Law and Gofpel may be feen more at large, and objections anfwered. As alfo in his Sermon on Gal. iii.* 24.

Law in all its rigour, and felt it was holy, just and good, or he would never have left his Father's bosom to die upon the Cross, to answer its demands. Antinomians, Neonomians, Arminians, &c. must all give up their various schemes, or, if they will be consistent with themselves, go off into open infidelity. For the Law in all its rigour is right, and glorious too, or the Son of God had never died to answer its demands. (1)

(1) *If Infidels triumph to see professed Christians advance such absurd and inconsistent schemes, they may do well to remember, that the very spirit of enmity to God and his Law, which produces these sad effects among professed Christians, hath led them still further, even to give up divine Revelation itself.*

Perhaps, first, *the Arminian spirit wrought in their hearts, and they were (in their own fancy) infallibly certain, that it is not just* that God should require more of his Creatures than they can do, and then damn them for not doing,—*The next step, they denied the* Atonement of Christ, *and commenced Socinians; for it appeared absolutely incredible, that the Son of God should die to answer the demands of an unjust Law.—But, lastly, when on further consideration, they find that the Old and New Testaments both join to teach, that* Cursed is every man that continueth not in all things written in the book of the Law to do them *(Deut. xxvii. 26.—Gal. iii, 10.) and find that it is asserted, that* Christ was made a curse for us, to redeem us from this very curse *(Ver. 13), even from the wrath to come, (*1 Thes. i. 10.*) and perceive, that the doctrine of Atonement is so universally inwrought into the whole of divine Revelation, that it cannot possibly be severed from it; and yet consider, that if Christ died to answer the demands of the Law, the Law must be supposed to be* holy, just and good, *in all its rigour; a point they never can believe: Therefore, to extricate themselves out of all difficulties at once, (bold, daring rebels to God, that they be!) notwithstanding all the infallible evidences God has given to its truth, they run the dreadful venture, to give up the Bible itself. They had rather turn professed Infidels, than own the divine Law to be* holy, just and good. *And then, so inconsistent are they, they pretend to make the* Law of Nature *their only rule. Not considering that their enmity to the* Law of Nature, *the true and real* Law of Nature, *hath driven them to this dreadful length.*

Ther. But, Sir, is not what some say, agreeable to Scripture, reason and experience, *viz.* that as our enmity against God arises from conceiving him to be our enemy, so we can never be reconciled to him, till we first see and are persuaded, that he loves us. (1)

Paul. With your leave, Sir, I will venture to affirm, that this scheme is contrary to Scripture, reason and the universal experience of all true Saints.—As to the experience of all true Saints, we have that in the plainest language, described by an inspired writer, 2 Cor. iii. 18. *We* ALL *with open face, beholding as in a glass the glory of the Lord, are changed into the same image.* A sight of the glory of God is what moves us to love him. Love to God is that image of God we are changed into. The image of God chiefly consists in love, as all own. And this is produced by a sense of God's glory, as the inspired Apostle affirms. —Besides, this scheme is contrary to the whole Tenor of Scripture, which every where teaches, that those who are enemies to God, are actually in a state of *condemnation* (Joh. iii. 18.) *and of Wrath*, (ver. 36.) and never can, nor will be received into the divine favour, till they *repent* and are *converted*, (Acts iii. 19.) *till they turn to God*, (Pov. i. 23, 24. —Ezek. xxxiii. 11.) and are *reconciled to him through Jesus Christ*. (2 Cor. v. 20—Luke xiii. 3, 5.) And indeed a true justifying Faith comprises all this in its very nature, in its very first act.—Besides if one should be so deluded, as to believe God was reconciled to him while impenitent, and out of Christ, this belief would not, could not bring him to love God. 'Tis true, such an one might, like the carnal Israelites at the side of the Red-Sea, be full of joy and love, arising merely from self-love. A kind of love,

The fool saith in his heart, there is no God. Did mankind really believe that there is a God of infinite Glory, they could not but be convinced that they are really under infinite obligations to love him as such, with all their hearts; and that the least defect deserves his everlasting wrath. But a fallen world are dead to God, blind to his beauty, and enemies to his Law; as all their reasonings, and all their conduct join to prove.—So that Atheism is the root of all errors; and enmity to God and his Law shuts our eyes against the Truth, and gives Infidelity a reigning power over our hearts·

(1) M. *p.* 25, 26, 27, 140.

which has in it nothing of the nature of true love to God: but is confiftent with a reigning enmity againft him.

Ther. But if our enmity againft God arifes from conceiving him to be our enemy, remove the caufe, and the effect will ceafe. If we view him as our reconciled Father and Friend, the occafion of our enmity being removed, our enmity will ceafe, and we fhall naturally love him.

Paul. Right, Theron, you fay true, if that be the only caufe of our enmity, this will effectually remove it. Nor fhall we need to be *born again* (John iii. 3.) or to have any new principle of *divine life* communicated to us. (John iii. 6—Eph. ii. 5.) But from the principles of Nature we may love God thus (Mat. v. 46.) and the regenerating, fanctifying influences of the holy Spirit will be wholly needlefs. The vail need not be taken from our hearts, that we may behold the Glory of God (2 Cor. iii. 18.) Only let God declare that he loves us and all is done. And if he was our enemy before we turned enemies to him, it feems proper and meet he fhould declare himfelf to be reconciled firft. Be fure, as this will put an end to the whole controverfy between him and us, and fet all things right. And one would think, that the God of peace would not be backward to make fuch a declaration, in the moft explicit manner, to all the human race, and that without the interpofition of a Mediator, if indeed he became an enemy to the human kind before we turned enemies to him. But if the human kind, without the leaft provocation turned enemies firft, and without any reafon revolted from their rightful Lord and Sovereign, and when God infinitely deferved their higheft love, joined in open rebellion with Satan, God's avowed foe; and if this, our infinitely unreafonable enmity is now the refult of the very temper of our whole heart, even of a fixed contrariety of nature to God, his Law and Government, which yet are faultlefs, yea, perfectly *holy, juft and good* (Rom. vii. 12. and viii. 7.) It is infinitely unreafonable that God fhould forgive us, till we acknowledge this is the cafe, and approve his Law, by which we ftand condemned, in the very bottom of our hearts. (Luke xviii. 13.) Nor, till we do this, can we poffibly look to God through Jefus Chrift for pardon, as abfolutely of mere free Grace. Without which, the Righteous Monarch of the Univerfe has declared, we never fhall be forgiven. (Rom. iii. 24.—Mar. xvi. 16.) But how contrary to reason is it, to suppose that God became enemy to the human kind first, and that all our enmity arises from conceiving him to be our enemy, as though some fault were originally on God's side, before we revolted from him. And so if he would now but become our friend and love us, we should love him without any more ado. What need then of the death of his Son? Or what need of the sanctifying influences of his Spirit? If he was our enemy first, he may well, without a Mediator, declare himself reconciled. And this will put an end to the whole controversy. A shocking scheme of Religion, this! But shocking as it is, and as reluctant as you may be, to own it in this shocking dress; yet you must, my Theron, adhere to it, if you would be consistent with yourself, or else give up your darling point. For if we are enemies to God, in the temper of our minds, previous to one thought of his being our enemy, a persuasion of his love, 'tis self evident, will never reconcile us to him.

Ther. Understand me right. If we were to love God primarily and chiefly for his own excellencies, a mere persuasion of his love to us, I own, would not be sufficient to bring us to this. But you are sensible, sir, that many look on this notion of loving God for himself, as a mere chimera. What makes God appear lovely to us, is a belief, an assured persuasion, that our sins are blotted out; and that God is our reconciled father and friend, and altogether love to us. (1)

Paul. But what warrant has a Christ-less sinner, while an enemy to God, to believe that his sins are blotted out? Or if he does believe so, and is ravished with his delusion, how can you prove this ravishment is of the nature of true Holiness? The Devil can thus delude and ravish a poor Sinner: But has Satan power to beget divine Grace, and real Holiness in the heart?

Ther. But if the Word of God is full on my side, this must determine the point.

Paul. Amen! I join issue here, with all my heart. Nor shall any other writings ever determine, for me, any of the doctrines of Religion.

Ther. It is expressly written, as the experience of all the Saints in the apostolic age, in 1 John iv. 16. *We have known*

(1) *M. p.* 266, 140.

and believed the love that God hath to us. And it follows in ver. 19. *We love him becauſe he firſt loved us.* In theſe two verſes our whole ſcheme is expreſſed in the plaineſt manner.

Paul. Yes, and it is as expreſsly written in James ii. 21. *Was not our Father Abraham juſtified by works?* And it is added, with reſpect to all good men, ver. 24. *Ye ſee then, how that by works a man is juſtified, and not by Faith only.* And in theſe two verſes our whole ſcheme, ſay the Arminians, is expreſſed in the plaineſt manner.

Ther. We are not to be carried away by the mere ſound of words in a ſingle text of Scripture or two, to notions contrary to the whole tenor of the ſacred volume. This is the way of Hereticks, who thus *wreſt the Scriptures to their own deſtruction.* (2 Pet. iii. 16.) We are rather by viewing the context, and comparing Scripture with Scripture, to ſearch for the true meaning of the inſpired writer. My dear Aſpaſio has ſet thoſe words of St. James in their proper light, and proved that they are not at all to the purpoſe of the Arminians, (Vol. 1. p. 268.) And indeed, I wonder how men that ever ſaw their own righteouſneſs to be as filthy rags, ſhould ever think of perverting the Apoſtle's words to a meaning, it is plain, he never intended.

Paul. You ſpeak well, my dear Theron, and I wonder how men, who are daily "with open face beholding as in a glaſs the glory of the Lord, and are changed into the ſame image from glory to glory, as by the Spirit of the Lord," ſhould ever think of putting ſuch a ſenſe on thoſe words of St. John. A ſenſe, it is plain, he never intended, neither came it into his heart. Indeed, I hope ſome men's hearts are more orthodox than their heads. However, let that be as it will; for it does not belong to you nor me to judge the ſtate of men's ſouls: God only knows their hearts: With God we leave them: Yet their notions of Religion we may examine, compare with Scripture, and paſs judgment upon. Here we have a good right to judge.—Wherefore, let us, obſerving the rules of interpreting Scripture, which you have hinted, rules which all parties muſt allow to be good: let us, I ſay, impartially examine thoſe words of the Apoſtle, in 1 John. iv. 16, 19, which you juſt now referred to, as clearly expreſſing your whole ſcheme.—Here my dear Theron, here is the bible; take it, and read the Epiſtle through; and when you have done, tell me—who are they, what is the character of the men who uſe this confident language: "We have known and believed the love that God hath to us." Were they Saints or Sinners? Did they know they were the children of God, or were they doubtful? Did they know they were in a good estate by being conscious of sanctifying operations in their own breasts?

Ther. I have read the Epistle—I grant they knew they were the children of God, and heirs of eternal Glory. —They did not merely hope this was the case; but they were certain of it: They KNEW it. (chap. iii. 1, 2.) And they knew it by such evidences as these. Because they knew God, loved him, and kept his commands, (chap. ii. 3, 4, 5.) imitated the example of Christ, (ver. 6.) loved the brethren, (ver. 10.) as bearing the image of God (chap. v. 1.) had overcome the Prince of Darkness (chap. ii. ver. 13.) were weaned from the world (ver. 15.) had such divine illuminations, as enabled them to understand, and confirmed them in the belief of the great doctrines of Religion, so that it was impossible they should be seduced (ver. 19, 27.) purified themselves after the pattern of Christ (chap. iii. 3.) lived in no sin, (ver. 6.) yea, could not live in sin (ver. 9.) made sanctification their criterion of a good estate, (ver. 10) looked upon all that were without it as children of the Devil (ver. 10.) they were governed by divine Grace in their conduct towards their brethren, (ver. 18, 19.) and made it their business to do the things which were pleasing in the sight of God: (ver. 22.) In a word, they were conscious to the sanctifying operations of God's Spirit, which dwelt in them (ver. 24.) &c. &c.

Paul. Now tell me, O my Theron, might not these men, on good grounds, and with a safe warrant, say, We have known and believed the love that God hath to us. They knew they were the children of God, and entitled to eternal glory. They knew they were of the number of the Elect, the sheep for whom Christ died with an absolute design to save. They knew all this, not by believing it without any evidence from Scripture, sense or reason; but they knew all this by evidences which pass for infallible in the court of Heaven: Evidences which they knew, and we know, the Judge will pronounce to be good and valid at the great day. Now tell me, O my Theron, if these men knew that God loved them, how can that prove, that Christ-less, impenitent sinners, enemies to God, unreconciled, can know it too? These men had good evidence for what they believ'd; but Christ-less sinners have no evidence that God loves them, or designs to save them, "from Scripture, sense or reason," as the celebrated Mr. Marshall is obliged to own. (1)

Ther. But the Apostle says, We love him because he first loved us. Which plainly supposes, they knew God loved them before they loved him.

Paul. If the Apostle, and all those Apostolic Saints, should join to declare they never understood the matter so, this would quite satisfy you. But which is altogether equivalent, they all agreed to make this their steady maxim: *He that committeth Sin is of the Devil.* (Chap. iii. 8, 9, 10.) But antecedent to the first act of Grace, they had only committed sin. Every act was a sinful act, before the first Gracious and holy act. And therefore, according to their own rule, they were not the children of God, but the children of the Devil; till they had performed, at least, one act of Grace. And until they knew they had performed an act of Grace according to their own rule, they could not know their state was changed for the better. But in the first act of saving Grace, the sinner's heart is really reconciled to God through Jesus Christ. So that we begin to love God before we know that he begins to love us— *Repent and be converted,* not because your sins are already, but that they *may be blotted out* (Acts iii. 19.)

Ther. This is not agreeable to my experience. (1st.) I had the love of God, as a reconciled God, manifested to my soul. (2nd.) Hereupon I believed that God was my reconciled God and Father. (3d.) And so I loved God because he first loved me. And indeed it is plain the Apostle taught, that God loves us before we love him. 1 John, iv. 10. *Not that we loved God, but that he loved us.* He loved us before we loved him.

Paul. But think a little, O my Theron! You do not maintain that a Sinner is actually entitled to the love of God, as his reconciled God and Father, before he believes in Christ. This is beyond all dispute inconsistent with the whole tenor of the Gospel. For unbelievers are *condemned* and under the *wrath of God* (John iii. 18, 36.) *We are justified by Faith, and not before Faith.* (Rom v. 1.)

Ther. As to Faith and Justification, I choose to defer

(1) M. p. 173.

these subjects to another time. But pray tell me; how do you understand these words?

Paul. As to the love of God towards us. There is (1st.) Electing love, whereby God *chose us in Christ to salvation before the foundation of the world.* (Eph. i. 4) (2nd.) Redeeming love towards the Elect, spoken of in 1 Joh. iv. 9, 10. *He loved us, and sent his Son to be the propitiation for our sins.* (3d.) There is the sovereign Grace and love of God, which is exercised in awakening, convincing and converting elect sinners. Eph. ii. 4, 5. *God, who is rich in mercy, for his great love wherewith he loved us, even when we were dead in sins, hath quickened us together with Christ. By Grace are ye saved.* (4th.) There is the love of God, as a reconciled Father, towards those that are converted and become his children, through Jesus Christ. Joh. xiv. 21. *He that hath my commandments and keepeth them, he it is that loveth me: And he that loveth me, shall be loved of my Father, and I will love him and manifest myself to him.* Ver. 23. *My Father will love him, and we will come unto him, and make our abode with him.* Rom. viii. 1. *There is therefore now no condemnation to them which are in Christ Jesus, who walk not after the Flesh, but after the Spirit.* Now the love of God, as a reconciled Father, none enjoy but those who are already the children of God; and they enjoy it, as our blessed Saviour teaches, in consequence of their loving him and keeping his commands. And such was the state of the Saints the Apostle John is speaking of. They knew that they were the children of God, and that they should be saved. And they lived daily in a sense of God's love, as their reconciled Father; for they loved God and kept his commands.

" But how came we to be in this blessed and happy state?" Might they say, " Once we were dead in sin, and enemies to God : Now with open face we behold as in a glass the glory of the Lord, and love him, and rejoice in his love. Once we were under condemnation and wrath : Now children of God, and heirs of eternal glory. Behold what manner of love the Father hath bestowed upon us, that we should be called the sons of God ! And whence is all this ? Not from any goodness in us, but of God's mere sovereign Grace. He loved us before we loved him; yea, before the foundation of the world. And we now love him becaufe he firſt loved us. Yea, we never fhould have loved him, had not he firſt loved us, and redeemed us by the blood of his Son, and quickened us when dead in ſin by his holy Spirit, and opened our eyes to behold his glory and beauty. Wherefore, feeing God is fo infinite in his love and goodneſs towards us, let us imitate him, and love one another."

Pray, my dear Theron, take your bible once more, and read from the 7th to the 21ſt verfe, in that ivth chap. of the 1ſt Epiſtle of John. Read the whole paragraph critically, and you may eafily fee, that this is the fum of the Apoſtle's reafonings. "*Beloved let us love one another.*— This is the duty I urge you to: and this is the argument I ufe. *God is Love.* And if we are born of God, if we are made partakers of his nature, we fhall love our Brother. If we do not love our Brother, our pretences to regeneration are a lie. If we do love our Brother, we are born of God; for *God is Love.* (fee ver. 7, 8, 11, 12, 13, 16, 20, 21.) That *God is Love,* is plain from the work of our Redemption by Chriſt. That the benevolence, love, and goodneſs of the divine nature is felf-moving, is plain, becaufe there was no goodnefs in us to move him to give his Son to die for us.—For we did not love God.—We were enemies.—God firſt loved us. Yea, if God had not pitied us in our loſt ſtate, and redeemed us, and brought us to know him, we fhould never have loved him. We love him now, but we never fhould have done fo, had not he firſt loved, redeemed, and converted us. Wherefore, full of gratitude, we love him becaufe he firſt loved us. And as the goodnefs of the divine Nature is thus felf-moving, and as God's heart is fo full of benevolence and love, and as we partake of the very fame nature by our new birth; fo we ſhould exercife it conſtantly in loving our brethren. The goodnefs of the divine Nature, as manifeſt in our Redemption, which is continually before our eyes, and its beauty which conſtantly affects our hearts, fhould change us into the fame image, and make us full of love to our brethren." (Ver. 7, 21.)

Ther. If, by the beauty of the divine Nature, you only mean, that God appears lovely, merely becaufe he loves us, I can underſtand you; and can love God on this account. But when you fpeak of loving God for himfelf, I know not what you mean, nor how it is possible for any to love God on this foot.

Paul. There is an essential difference between being charmed with the beauty of the divine Goodness, and being ravished merely to think that God loves me. The one will infallibly change us into the divine Image, agreeable to Mat. v. 44, 45, 48; the other will never raise us higher than to the Publican's standard, ver. 46, 47.

Besides, my dear Theron, tell me; do you verily believe, that it is more to God's honor to be your particular friend, than it is to be by NATURE GOD? Does his friendship to you make him shine brighter, than all the infinite GLORIES OF HIS ETERNAL GODHEAD? And is he more worthy to be loved and worshiped because he loves you, than for his own REAL DIVINITY? Or, as the Papists cannonize saints for their extraordinary attachment to the Roman Church, and then pay them religious worship; so do you deify God, for being your particular friend, and give him divine worship merely on this account; but for which you would be full of " hatred and heart-risings against him?" We use to think divine love and worship ought by no means to be paid to a mere creature, how kind soever to us. But if you leave DIVINITY, if you leave the GLORY OF THE DIVINE MAJESTY as he is in himself, out of the account; and love and worship him merely for his love to you, and make him your GOD, merely for that; and so pay him divine worship not because he is by NATURE GOD, but because he is your particular friend; how will you free yourself from the guilt of idolatry?—To be sure, you are so far from paying a proper regard to real Divinity, that you shew yourself quite blind to his beauty and glory, and stupid to that which charms all the heavenly world. And in their eyes, you must appear in a very selfish, impious, contemptible light, in your highest raptures.

Had Nicaulis, the Queen of Sheba, on her return from King Solomon's court, in all her conversation, dwelt only on the royal bounty which he gave her, (1 Kin. x. 13.) and expressed her love to him on this account alone, wondering how any man of sense could talk of the fine and charming accomplishments of the King, and what they meant by loving him primarily and chiefly on the foot of his own personal merit: would not those gentlemen who had been her attendants in her tour to Jerusalem, have been tempted to look upon her as a person of no taste, that the fine and charming accomplishments of even Solomon, in all his glory, could not touch her heart. And I dare say, her name would not have been mentioned in the Jewish history, unless with infamy. But what was Solomon's glory, compared with the glory of the King of the whole universe!

What would the Queen of Israel have thought, had the daughters of Jerusalem said unto her, "What is thy beloved more than another beloved, O thou fairest among women?" Would she not have soon replied, with the fervor of an ardent lover? *My beloved is white and ruddy, the chiefest among ten thousand; yea, he is altogether lovely*. Cant. v. 9, 10, 16. And have not the regenerate infinitely more reason to adopt this language? For as natural men have by nature a taste to the beauties of the natural world; so spiritual men have by grace a taste to the beauties of the moral world. As King Solomon appeared exceeding glorious to the Queen of Sheba; so the Lord Jehovah who sits on a *Throne high and lifted up, as the thrice holy Monarch of the universe*, appears exceeding glorious, not only to Angels in Heaven, but to Saints on Earth, (Isa. vi. 3.—2 Cor. iii. 18.) And they are all ready in the language of the Queen of Sheba, to say, *Happy are thy men, happy are these thy servants, which stand continually before thee.* (1 Kin. x. 8.) The infinite amiableness of God, as he is in himself, is the chief source of the refined joys of the heavenly world. To behold such a God, to love and be beloved by him, is the Heaven of Heaven itself. And the more exalted his glory and beauty, the sweeter their love and joy. His being *what he is in himself*, so infinitely desirable, renders it so infinitely happifying to them, to enjoy him for ever as their own, Psal. lxxiii. 25.

Ther. Perhaps there may be more in what you plead for than I have been wont to think. And as I design fully to consider these things, that I may be under the best advantages to make up a right judgment, pray point out some of the chief differences between these two kinds of love to God.

Paul. (1st.) If I love God for himself, God, even God himself is the object beloved: And the act by me performed, is properly an act of love to God. If I love God merely because he loves me, I am the object really beloved: And the act is properly an act of self-love. (2d.) The one supposes the glory and amiableness of the divine Nature is really seen: The other may be where the heart is wholly blind to this kind of beauty, as it does not arise from a sense of God's amiableness, but altogether from selfish considerations.—(3d.) If God is loved for himself, the whole of God's law and government will also be loved, as in themselves *beautiful, holy, just* and *good*, a transcript and image of God's nature. If God is loved merely because he loves me, I shall be reconciled to God's Law and Government only as considering myself safe from the stroke of divine justice. And I shall be reconciled to God's decrees only as considering them in my favour. Not really caring what becomes of the rest of my fellow men, I shall pretend to like God's plan of government as being safe myself, but for which, I should, as your Author expresses it, be full of "hatred and heart-risings in spite of my heart." (1) If God is loved for himself, every thing which bears his image, will, for the same reason, be loved, as being in itself lovely, as resembling the standard of true beauty: But otherwise, all my love towards all other things of a religious nature, will be merely selfish.—For instance, I shall love the children of God merely on selfish accounts; as, because they love me, belong to my party, &c. So the hypocritical Galatians once loved St. Paul, as they thought he had been the means of their conversion; but when he was afterwards obliged to tell them some truths which they disrelished, their love grew cold; yea, they rather inclined to join with the false teachers, his avowed enemies who were constantly endeavouring to undermine that scheme of Religion which was dearer to him than his life. This proved they never really loved Paul himself; who still continued the same he was before. So the Israelites seemed to love God, much, at the side of the Red-Sea, while they thought he loved them; but the waters of Marah soon brought them to different feelings.—(4th) If God is loved for himself, it will be natural to imitate him, and delight to please him. For we always love to imitate and please those who are really dear to us, and their *commands are not grievous*. (1 Joh. v. 3.) But you know the character of the men, *who*

(1) M. p. 24, 25, 140.

sang God's praise, but *soon forgat his works*. (Psal. cvi. 12, 13.) And *forty years long was he grieved with this generation.* (Psal. xcv. 10.) They were much engaged to have themselves pleased; but cared not what became of God's honour, when they were crossed. (5th) If God is loved for himself, then the enjoyment of God will be our highest happiness. *Whom have I in Heaven but thee?—And there is none upon earth that I desire besides thee.* (Psal. lxxiii. 25.) Whereas, if we love God only in a firm persuasion of his love to us, as himself cannot be our portion, so we shall naturally seek rest elsewhere. For nothing can be a portion to our souls, which is not loved for itself.—The man that marries merely for money, cannot expect to find that delight and satisfaction in his companion, which he might in a person agreeable to his taste. And no wonder he absents himself from her company, and contrives excuses to justify himself. Wherefore, (6th) If God is loved for himself, as there is thereby a foundation laid for a conformity to him in the temper of our minds, and a life of communion with him; so hereby it may be discovered, that we, thus bearing his image are really his children.—And so an assurance of our good estate may be obtained from our sanctification; which on the other scheme never can, if we will be honest to our own souls. As well may the rush grow without mire, and the flag without water; yea, as well may you build a cathedral on the stalk of a tulip, says your Aspasio, (1) as one in your scheme maintain assurance from a conscioufness of his own sanctification.

Here, my dear Aspasio, the conversation stopped.—I sat silent, all my thoughts turned inward.—" O my soul," said I to myself, " this is my very case. My sanctification has for a long time, been no more to be seen than the stars at noon. I have found by sad experience, no assurance could possibly be obtained this way. To seek assurance by marks and signs of Grace, only cherishes my doubts, and increases my perplexity. And what if this is indeed the very reason, that really I never had any true Grace?"——I was shocked—my heart recoiled—" O dreadful!—an heir of Hell! after all my high raised hopes!"

Thus I sat silent several minutes, quite lost in self reflection, till Paulinus began again to speak.—" I must dismiss

(1) *D. p.* 360, 362.

these subjects at present," said I, "and retire. Your thoughts on the remaining points, I hope to hear at a more convenient season." Paulinus replied, "When you please, Sir, I am at your service." "To-morrow evening I will wait upon you," said I.—After he had expressed many kind wishes for my good, and I had asked his prayers, I retired to my closet. And, O my Aspasio, you may easily guess how I spent the night. For *the wicked are like the troubled sea, when it cannot rest, whose waters cast up mire and dirt.*"

DIALOGUE II.

Tuesday Evening, December 12, 1758.

I RETURNED at the appointed time. And after some agreeable conversation on general subjects, I introduced the SECOND QUESTION.—But Paulinus insisted I should tell my opinion first—which I did, in the very words of the best writers I had seen.—Thus we begun.—

Paul. Pray, tell me exactly, what *justifying* Faith is, in your opinion?

Ther. "It is a real persuasion in my heart, that Jesus Christ is mine, and that I shall have life and salvation by him; that whatsoever Christ did for the redemption of mankind, he did it for me. Faith is an hearty assurance, that our sins are freely forgiven us in Christ.—Justifying Faith hath for the special object of it, forgiveness of sins.—A man doth not believe that his sins are forgiven him already, before the act of believing; but that he shall have forgiveness of sins. In the very act of justification, he believes his sins are forgiven him; and so receives forgiveness. (1)—Faith is a real persuasion that the blessed Jesus

(1) *Marrow of Mod. Div. with Notes.* p. 158, 273.

N. B. Wendelinus is the author of the last mentioned Definition of Faith; who is one of the authorities Mr. Hervey refers to. (D. p. 315.) *And as this Definition seems to have been made with care, and to be very exact; so it is worthy*

hath shed his blood for me, fulfilled all righteousness in my stead; that through his great atonement and glorious obedience, he has purchased even for my sinful soul, reconciliation with God, sanctifying grace, and all spiritual blessings." And the language of Faith is this; "Pardon is mine, grace is mine, Christ and all his spiritual blessings are mine.—God has freely loved me; Christ has graciously died for me; and the Holy Ghost will assuredly sanctify me in the belief, the appropriating belief, of these precious truths." This appropriating and taking home to myself the blessings of the Gospel is of the essence of Faith. (1) " It is not a persuasion, that we have already received Christ and his salvation, or that we have been already brought into a state of Grace: But only that God is pleased graciously to give Christ and his salvation unto us, to bring us into a state of Grace. (2) To sum up all in a word: Faith is a persuasion, that I am one for whom Christ died with a design to save; that God is reconciled to me, loves me, and will save me. And all this is believed by the direct act of Faith, antecedent to any reflection. (3)

Paul. O my Theron, be you not mistaken? Is not Faith usually called *coming to Christ, receiving Christ, trusting in Christ, believing in Christ, flying to Christ?* &c.

Ther. It is. But this is an after act, and is built upon the former. *First,* I believe, that pardon, grace, Christ and all his spiritual blessings are mine: And then I trust I shall assuredly be saved by Christ.—*First,* I believe that Christ died for me in particular, and that God is my God; and this encourages me to come to Christ and trust in him. If I did not know that Christ loves me, I should not dare to trust in him. (4) Wherefore, in the first direct act of Faith, I believe that God " is reconciled to me," (5) that Christ has " rescued me from Hell," and " established my title to all the blessings included in the promises." (6) Just as my tenant believed

of particular attention.——My sins are not forgiven, but I believe they are forgiven, and so receive forgiveness; i. e. *I knew it was not true, but I believed it to be true, and so it became true.* Which exactly answers to the account Mr. Marshal gives of Faith. Of which more presently.

(1) D. *p.* 296, 362, 345, 315.   (2) M. *p.* 176.   (3) D. *p.* 358, 359.   (4) D. *p.* 312, 313.   (5) D. *p.* 169. (6) D. *p.* 181.

me, when once I sent him word, "that I had cancelled his bond and forgiven his debt. (1) Just as my servant believed me, when I freely gave him a little farm. (2) And just as you believed the estate your own, which was bequeathed to you in your late father's last will. You first believed your title good, and then took possession of it as your own. (3) I am sensible, this is not what is called the orthodox opinion; it is more " refined and exalted," (4) and more exactly agreeable to the truth. (5)

Paul. But my dear Theron, how do you know that Christ, pardon, grace and glory are your's? What evidence have you for your belief? A belief, on which you venture your precious soul for a whole eternity.

Ther. The holy scripture clears up my title, (6) and enables me to appropriate to myself in particular, what is given, granted and made over in the written word to sinners in general. (7) To explain myself, it is written in Isa. ix. 6. *To us a Son is given.* (8) Isa. liii. 6. *The Lord hath laid on him the iniquities of us all.* (9) 1 Cor. xv. 1. *Christ died for our sins.* (10) John vi. 32. *My father giveth you the true bread from Heaven.* (11) 1 John v 9. *This is the Record, that God hath given to us eternal life.* (12) Acts xiii 28. *Unto you is preached the forgiveness of sins.* (13) Isa. xliii. 25. *I, even I, am he, that blotteth out thy transgressions.* (14) And by Faith I appropriate all this to myself. I believe that Christ is mine, given to me in particular: My sins in particular were laid on him: He died for my sins in particular: He is my bread: Eternal life is mine: My sins are forgiven: My transgressions are blotted out. And so according to Scripture, *I believe the love that God hath to me.* 1 Joh. iv. 16. *I believe I shall be saved.* Act, xv 11. *I believe Christ loved me, and gave himself for me.* Gal. ii. 20. (15) With Thomas I say, *My Lord, my God!* Joh. xx. 28. "I am persuaded in my heart, that Jesus is my Lord, who bought me with his blood: That Jesus is my God, who will exert all his adorable perfections for my good. (16) This is Faith, according to the common acceptation of the

(1) D. *p.* 298. (2) D. *p.* 273. (3) D. *p.* 255. (4) D. *p.* 295. (5) D. *p.* 312, 313, 334, 335. (6) D. *p.* 295. (7) D. *p.* 305, 314. (8) D. *p.* 308. (9) D. *p.* 304. (10) D. *p.* 318. (11) D. *p.* 307. (12) D. *p.* 319. (13) D. *p.* 303. (14) D. *p.* 329. (15) D. *p.* 326, (16) D. *p.* 330.

word believe. (1) And this Faith our Saviour himself, allows to be genuine. (2) And if I should not thus believe, I should make God a liar. (3)

Paul. How make God a liar, my dear Theron? Hath God said that Christ died with an absolute design to save all mankind? And hath God expresly declared, that he will save them all? That you think yourself obliged in conscience, while out of Christ, to believe he died with an absolute design to save you, and that God will certainly save you; and that it would be no better than making God a liar, not to believe so.

Ther. No, no; God hath never said any such thing, expresly or implicitly. Yea, God has plainly enough declared, that Christ died with an absolute design to save only the Elect; and that in fact, no other ever will be saved. This we are all agreed in. (4)

Paul. did you know then that you was one of the Elect, before you believed? That you thought yourself bound in conscience to believe that you should be saved; left otherwise, you should be guilty of so horrible a sin, as to make God a liar.

Ther. No, by no means. For no man can know his election till after Faith and Justification.

Paul. How then could you make God a liar? Is it any where declared in his written word, that your sins in particular are forgiven, and that you shall be saved.

Ther. No; so far from it, that before I believed my sins were forgiven, they were in fact not forgiven: But I was under condemnation and wrath.

Paul. But surely here is some great mystery. You say, you believe that Christ died with a design to save only the Elect, and that you did not know that you was Elected; and yet you believed that Christ died with a design to save you. You say, your sins were not forgiven before you believed; and yet you believed they were forgiven. You seem, my friend, to be so far from any danger of making God a liar by not believing; that rather you make him a liar by believing your sins are forgiven, when God says

(1) D. *p.* 297. (2) D. *p.* 330. (3) D. *p.* 354.
(4) *Boston on the Two Covenants, p.* 27, 34. *N. B. He says, Isa. liii. 6. (a text Theron just now applied to himself) respects only the elect, p.* 30.

they are not. At least, to make the best of it, I do not see what evidence you have for your belief. Nay, how can such a Faith as yours possibly be the result of evidence, and of a rational conviction? For the case does not seem to admit of any evidence. For how can there be any evidence to prove the truth of that which as yet is not true? Pray, unfold this riddle, like a right honest man, and tell me the secret of the whole affair.

Ther. This matter is honestly stated, and that with great exactness, in Mr. Mushall's Gospel Mystery; a book, my Aspasio values next to the Bible. (1) These are the very words of that celebrated author. "Let it be well observed, that the reason why we are to assure ourselves in our Faith, that God freely giveth Christ and his salvation to us in particular, is not because it is a truth before we believe it, but because it becometh a certain truth when we believe; and because it never will be true, except we do in some measure, persuade and assure ourselves that it is so. We have no absolute promise or declaration in Scripture, that God certainly will, or doth give Christ and his salvation, to any one of us in particular; neither do we know it to be true already by Scripture, or sense, or reason, before we assure ourselves absolutely of it: Yea, we are without Christ's salvation at present, in a state of sin and misery, under the curse and wrath of God. Only we are bound by the command of God, thus to assure ourselves: And the Scripture doth sufficiently warrant us, that we shall not deceive ourselves, in believing a lie: But *according to our Faith, so shall it be to us.*" Mat. ix. 29. (N. B.) "This is a strange kind of assurance, far different from other ordinary kinds; and therefore, no wonder if it be found weak and imperfect, and difficult to be obtained, and assaulted with many doubtings. We are constrained to believe other things on the clear evidence we have that they are true, and would remain true, whether we believe them or no; so that we cannot deny our assent, without rebelling against the light of our senses, reason, or conscience. But here our assurance is not impressed on our thoughts by any evidence of the thing; but we must work it out in ourselves by the assistance of the Spirit of God." (2) Labouring for it, as my dear Aspasio explains

(1) D. *p.* 336.   (2) M. *p.* 173, 174.

the words, "inceſſantly and aſſiduouſly, 'till our Lord come." (1) *What things ſoever ye deſire when ye pray, believe that ye receive them, and ye ſhall have them. Mar. ix.* 24 (2)

(1) M. *Preface, p.* 7.

(2) *Reader ſtop and think a minute.*—What is it, that we are thus to aſſure ourſelves of, without any evidence from Scripture, or ſenſe, or reaſon? That God ſo loved the world, as to give his only begotten Son, that whoſoever believeth in him, ſhould not periſh, but have everlaſting life? No: for this is true before we believe it, and whether we believe it or not. And it is a truth plainly taught in Scripture.—What then? "That God freely giveth Chriſt and his ſalvation to me in particular," according to Mr. Marſhal. That "pardon is mine, grace is mine, Chriſt and all his ſpiritual bleſſings are mine," as Mr. Hervey expreſſes it.—And now it is true enough, this is "*not* declared in Scripture; is *not* true before we believe it; and we muſt believe without any evidence from Scripture, ſenſe or reaſon." Thus the point is ſtated in a book Mr. Hervey approves of next to the Bible.

Objection. "No," ſays Mr. Gellatly, a great admirer of Mr. Hervey, "no ſuch thing. We do not believe we have a ſaving intereſt in Chriſt. We only believe we have a common intereſt. A ſaving intereſt is not made over to us in the Goſpel Grant: But a common intereſt is ours by a free deed of gift. Wherefore I believe I have a common intereſt, I claim it, I demand it, I take poſſeſſion of it as my own. And this is Faith. (See Mr. Gel. Obſervations, &c. p. 76, 88.)

Anſwer. You claim, you take poſſeſſion—Of what? my friend! Of a common intereſt.—This is your's, you ſay.—This you claim, this you poſſeſs—And this is ALL.—A common intereſt, and no more.—You claim no more, and you can have no more on this foot. For you acknowledge, your deed of gift conveys no more—But Meſſrs. Harvey and Morſhal claim more. They take poſſeſſion of a ſaving intereſt as their own. And therefore honeſtly confeſs, they have no evidence from Scripture, ſenſe or reaſon. And if Mr. G. ſhould venture to put in as high a claim, I hope he will make as honeſt a Conceſſion.

Objection. "'Tis." But "I believe that Chriſt is mine, and that I ſhall have Life and Salvation by him." P. 103.

Anſwer. "Salvation!"—But this is a ſaving intereſt, or made over in your deed of gift, as you own. The bible no

Paul. I have on the table a paper containing twelve short queries, relative to the point in hand. If it is not disagreeable, I will read it to you.

Ther. If you please, Sir, I should be glad to hear it.

Paul. It was wrote this very day, on reading that remarkable passage in Mr. Marshal, you have just recited, and on a general view of the controversy, as stated by him, and by your friend Aspasio, and as expecting to see you this evening.

TWELVE QUERIES.

Quer. 1. Did God ever require any one of the sons of Adam to believe any proposition to be true, unless it was in fact true, before he believed it? We are required to believe, there is a God—that Christ is the Son of God—that he died for sinners—that he sent his Apostles to preach the Gospel to every creature—that he that believeth shall be saved—that he that believeth not, shall be damned—that without holiness no man shall see the Lord: In a word, we are required to believe all the truths taught in the *bible.*— But then, they are all true, before we believe them, and whether we believe them, or not.

Quer. 2. Are not all these truths contained in the Scriptures of the Old and New Testament, which it is necessary for us to know and believe in order to our salvation? Is not this a point which has ever been strenuously maintained

where declares, that you in particular " shall have life and salvation." You believe now " without any evidence from Scripture sense or reason," just as Mr. Marshal says. So I see, your Faith is the same as his; but he is frank and open-hearted, and tells the honest truth to the world.

Object. *But if a common interest in Christ, and salvation are mine, by the free and absolute grant of the Gospel; this gives me a warrant, by Faith, to claim and take possession of Christ and salvation as my own for ever: i. e. to believe that Christ is mine, and that I shall have life and salvation by him. (p.* 88, 90.)

Ans. That is, if *a* common interest *is mine, this gives me a warrant to believe a* saving interest *is mine. And so according to* Mr. Marshal, *" though a* saving interest *is not mine, before I believe ; yet if I believe it is mine, then it will be mine."*
—*But of this more presently.*

by all Proteſtants? But are they not all true, before we believe them, and whether we believe them, or not?

Quer. 3, Is it ſafe to venture our ſouls for eternity, merely on the truth of a propoſition no where contained in the bible? "Theron, Chriſt died for thee in particular, and thy ſins are forgiven." Is this propoſition contained in the bible? Is it taught in ſcripture? If it had been, would it not have been true, before it was believed? and whether it was ever believed or no?—If Theron ventures his ſoul upon the truth of this propoſition, and finds himſelf at laſt deceived, can he blame the bible? Was it contained in that book? Did he learn it thence?—Nay, he owns he did not. But then he thinks God has required him to work up himſelf to ſuch a belief, and promiſed, that *according to his Faith, ſo ſhall it be unto him*. And yet owns, he has no evidence of the thing from Scripture, ſenſe or reaſon.

Quer. 4. Did God ever require any one of the ſons of Adam, to believe any thing to be true, without ſufficient previous evidence that it was true?—Look through the bible.—Where ſhall we find one inſtance?—Not in the Old Teſtament—nor in the New Teſtament—no, not even in one of theſe particulars, theſe writers uſually refer to, to illuſtrate and confirm this "ſtrange kind of aſſurance."

Not in Abraham, who *againſt Hope believed in Hope*, that he ſhould have a ſon; Sarah being not only barren, but paſt the age of child-bearing. For he had ſufficient evidence for the thing he believed: Even the known, the plain, the expreſs promiſe of the God of Truth. (1)

Not in the Iſraelites, who left Egypt, ſet out for Canaan, but *could not enter in becauſe of unbelief*. For they had ſufficient evidence to believe, that God was able and willing to do all that he had engaged. (2) And that if they would

---

(1) D. *p.* 191, 355.

(2) *God's promiſe, Exod.* iii. 17, *to bring the Iſraelites to Canaan, did not abſolutely oblige him to bring every individual man, woman and child there. Some might die by the way; and yet God not be a liar. Exod. xxxii.* 27, 28. *Yea many did die by the way; and yet it is* impoſſible *for God to lie. Heb. vi.* 13. *That phraſe in Numbers xiv.* 34, *proves that God did not think himſelf bound by his promiſe to bring them every one there, let them be ever ſo perverſe. But if God was not abſolutely obliged to bring every one there, then no one in particular,*

truſt his wiſdom, power, goodneſs and fidelity, be at his beck, and march under his banner, and *wholly follow him*, (Num. xxxii. 11.) they might ſafely enter, and eaſily conquer the country, although their *walls were built up to Heaven and the ſons of Anak were there.*——

Not in David—who believed that he ſhould be king of Iſrael; for he had ſufficient evidence for his belief, from the expreſs promiſe of Almighty God. (1)

Not in the pious Jews in Babylon. (Iſa. i. 10.) For although they could not ſee the leaſt probability, from outward appearances, of their return to their beloved Zion; yet they had a good warrant to truſt in the Lord, and ſtay themſelves upon their God, who was able and who had expreſsly and abſolutely promiſed, at the end of ſeventy years, to bring them back. (2)

Nor in Peter walking on the water. For he had ſufficient evidence, from Chriſt's commanding him to come to him, to believe that Chriſt would keep him from ſinking. (3)

Nor in the Diſciples—ſo often upbraided for their unbelief of Chriſt's Reſurrection. For they had ſufficient evidence that he was riſen. (4) Nor in thoſe who had the Faith of miracles, and could ſay to this mountain, *Be thou removed and caſt into the ſea;* for they had ſufficient evidence, to believe it would be done, reſulting from Chriſt's expreſs promiſe in the caſe. When they were called to work miracles in confirmation of the Chriſtian Religion, they had not the leaſt reaſon to doubt in their hearts, but that he who had authoriſed them, would, for his honour's ſake, and for his word's ſake, perform the miracles, which

when they ſet out from Egypt, had ſufficient warrant to believe, and ſay, " I ſhall get to Canaan: I know I ſhall: God has promiſed, and I ſhould make him a liar, if I did not believe, that I, in particular, ſhould get ſafe there." After that declaration in Num. xiv. 31. Caleb and Joſhua had a good warrant for ſuch a belief. And ſo, after we know we are united to Chriſt by a true and lively Faith, we may be certain, that we ſhall get ſafe to Heaven at laſt. Job. iii. 16. and v. 24. But not before: as there is no abſolute promiſe of ſalvation to all mankind. Gal. iii. 29 Job. iii. 18. Rom. ix. 15, 21. 2 Cor. i. 20. Compare Joſh. i. 6. with Joſh. vii. 5. and Heb. vi. 18. See alſo Num. xxxii. 15.

(1) D. p. 324, 357, 362. (2) D. p. 321. (3) D. p. 331. (4) D. p. 355, 356.

they were inspired to declare should be done.(1)—Nor in those who came to Christ to be healed. For they had sufficient evidence, to believe that Christ was able to do it. (2) Nor indeed is there one instance in the bible, of God's requiring a man to believe any thing whatsoever, without sufficient previous evidence of its truth.

How incredible, therefore! how infinitely incredible is it! That God should first put the Bible into our hands, as rational creatures, and charge us strictly to adhere to it on pain of Eternal Damnation; (Rev. xxii. 18.) and then suspend the eternal salvation of all mankind on their believing a thing to be true, no where contained in the bible; yea, of the truth of which they have no evidence, from "Scripture, sense or reason; yea, which, as yet, is not true, but flatly contradictory to divine revelation: and sentence men to eternal damnation, for not believing, what they would be glad to believe with all their hearts, had they sufficient evidence of its truth! For there is no man but would be glad to know, that instead of the eternal torments of Hell, he should have the eternal joys of Heaven.(3)

Quer. 5. Is not this the difference between faith and presumption, as the words are commonly understood among

(1) *M. p.* 174. (2) *M. p.* 173.

(3) *Some, who are in this scheme, pretend to be great enemies to* carnal reason. *But they must renounce all reason, and the bible too, or one would think, they never can be full proof against conviction.—But they say, we must become fools for Christ. But do they really think, that Christianity is, in fact, a foolish religion? Christianity, which is the wisdom of God: and which exhibits a most exact picture of all the divine perfections; a picture a most infinitely brighter than that which was given in the creation of the world. The work of our Redemption is the master-piece of all God's works, and Christianity the brightest display of all Gods perfections. Its wisdom, glory and beauty are such, as gain the attention of all the exalted genius's of the Heavenly world.*—1 Pet. i. 12. *What an infinite reproach to God and his Son is it then, for us mortals, to misrepresent this rational, divine and glorious religion, so as to make it, in fact, one of the most foolish, inconsistent and absurd things imaginable! and then, to hide the shame of its nakedness raise an outcry about carnal reason!— by this means, many poor sinners have been early led to look upon*

mankind, viz. that in the one, we believe because we have sufficient evidence, in the other, without any evidence at all? And is not this the constant character of all self-deceived hypocrites, that they have "a real persuasion in their hearts" of the love of God to their souls, and a confident expectation of eternal life, without any real evidence?— Mat. vii. 21, 27. Luk. xiii. 25, 26, 27. and xviii. 9 11.

Quer. 6. Is not this faith analogous to that which the Devil tempted our Saviour to exercise? when (Lu. iv. 8) *He brought him to Jerusalem, and set him on a pinnacle of the temple, and said unto him, if thou be the Son of God, cast thyself down from hence: For it is written,* (Psal. xci. 11.) *He shall give his angels charge over thee, to keep thee, and in their hands they shall hold thee up, lest at any time thou dash thy*

experimental religion, as a silly, foolish thing; although, in reality there is nothing in it, but what is as rational as the mathematicks.—Yea, if true religion were not perfectly rational, how could it please the infinitely wise God, who is the fountain and source of all reason? how could it be suited to raise, exalt, and ennoble rational creatures? or how could it deserve to be called by the name of WISDOM, by Solomon the wisest of men?

Object. "But if the religion of the bible is so rational a thing, why are not Socinians, Pelagians, &c. pleased with it, who so greatly cry up reason?"

Answ. Merely because it is so contrary to the darling corruptions of their hearts. Our blessed Saviour, who well understood human nature, and the nature of his own religion, affirms that this is the true cause, Joh. iii. 19, 20, 21. Had they but good hearts, they would be charmed with the wisdom and glory of the Christian religion, (Joh. viii. 47.) even as the inhabitants of Heaven be, Eph. iii. 10.—For after all their glorying, their own schemes, although a little better glossed over, yet in reality are as inconsistent and absurd, as this that Theron pleads for.—In the apostolic age, divine truths were set in so clear a light, that the worst of hereticks were obliged, were necessitated to see, that they were inconsistent with themselves; and so were forced to be self-condemned; as is plainly implied in Tit. iii. 10, 11. An heretick, after the first and second admonition, reject: knowing that he that is such, is subverted, and sinneth, being CONDEMNED OF HIMSELF.—And, no doubt, there is light enough, in the holy Scrip-

foot against a stone.—Here was a promise, a precious promise out of God's own word. And *he that believeth not God, hath made him a liar.* The Devil urged our Saviour to appropriate, and take it home to himself in particular: And be verily "persuaded in his heart" he should be safe, although he cast himself down.—However, on a critical examination of the text the Devil recited, there could be no evidence from that, of safety to Christ, if he had cast himself down.—So therefore he must believe really without any evidence from "Scripture, sense or reason;" and the Devil would have had him think, that according to his Faith, so should it be to him.

Quer. 7. If the Devil attempted thus to delude our blessed Saviour himself, by misapplying a precious promise, has he not courage?—Has he not power?—Has he not will?—to attempt to delude poor sinners in a like manner; that thereby, Devil as he is, he may accomplish their eternal ruin! And are we not forewarned from Heaven, of a false spirit, and charged not to believe every spirit? (1 Joh. iv. 1.) For that *Satan himself is transformed into an Angel of light.* (2 Cor. xi. 14.)

Quer. 8. Did ever Christ or his apostles define Faith to be "a real persuasion that Christ died for me in particular, and that pardon, Grace and glory are mine?" They call it coming to Christ, receiving Christ, trusting in Christ, believing in Christ, believing on Christ. &c. but never call it, believing Christ is mine, and that my sins are forgiven. It is true, the Saints in the Old Testament, and in the New, usually speak the language of assurance. And it is as true, they had sufficient evidence of their good estate from their sanctification. This was their evidence. They knew no other. All who pretended to belong to Christ without this, were branded for liars. (1. Joh. ii. 4.) But where do we ever read of their endeavouring to work up themselves to an assurance, professedly without any evidence?

tures, to produce the same still, were it brought out, and held before the eyes of hereticks in this age, 2 Tim. iii. 16, 17 — *For the truth, and only the truth, is, or can be, universally consistent: but all false schemes, follow them up, will appear to be inconsistent. Reason is wholly on the side of truth. And true religion is the only religion, that is perfectly rational and consistent throughout.*

Quer. 9. Is there one in all St. Paul's catalogue of believers in Heb. xi. whose faith consisted in believing without any evidence? (1)

Quer. 10. Were ever any awakened sinners invited and urged to believe, by Christ, or his Apostle, and told at the same time, that the thing they were to believe, was not true as yet? Nor had they any evidence from Scripture, sense or reason, it ever would be true; but however most solemnly assured by the promise and oath of God, if they would venture to believe without any evidence at all in the case it should be according to their faith.—Was this the thing the Apostles dwelt upon in all their preaching? Was this the thing they urged awakened sinners to, with all their might? No: they never heard of it—neither came it into their hearts, to think that this was justifying faith.

Quer. 11. Is not the thing believed a lie? It was not true, before it was believed, as is granted. But believing an untruth, to be true, cannot make it true.—It cannot, according to reason—It cannot, according to Scripture—It cannot, according to experience. It was never known, since the world began, to produce this effect in any one instance; unless in this case. And we have no evidence from Scripture, sense or reason, that it ever did in this.

Quer. 12. Is it not astonishing, and one of the most unaccountable things in the world, that a rational creature, with the Bible in his hands, should ever be able to work up himself to believe, what he knows is not yet true; and what he knows, he has no evidence, that it ever will be true? No wonder, these men are so much troubled with doubts.—No wonder, they are afraid, they believe a lie—No wonder, they are obliged so much to strive and struggle against this unbelief; a kind of unbelief we no where read of in the Bible. A kind of conflict, no Saint ever had, that stands on Scripture record; as themselves are obliged to own.(2) To struggle daily to believe, without any evidence from Scripture, sense, or reason! to have *this*, for their Christian conflict! an unheard of conflict in the Apostolic age! Instead of struggling against this kind of unbelief, Scripture, sense and reason, all join to justify it. As nothing can be plainer than that we ought never to believe any thing, with more confidence, than in exact proportion

(1) D. *p.* 326. (2) M. *p.* 186.

to our evidence. To do otherwise, and that professedly, is the most presumptuous thing in the world. And to think, by being thus strong in the Faith, we shall give glory to God, is the very first-born of delusion, that even Satan himself ever begot in the heart of a fallen creature.(1)

(1) D. *p.* 355, 342, 343, 369. *Wendelinus and other ancient and modern writers, without the least scruple, say, that, in the direct act of justifying Faith, I believe " my sins are forgiven"—" God is reconciled to me," &c. &c. Others who seem to be in the same scheme, are more cautious in their expressions; and, to avoid the charge of " believing a lie," they word themselves so ambiguously, that it is very difficult to know what they mean. For it has often been urged against this scheme, " If faith consists in believing my sins are forgiven, then they are forgiven before I believe, or else I believe a lie."—And it is wonderful, to see what methods have been taken by writers to avoid this difficulty.—However, when all is said and done, there are in Nature but these three ways to solve the difficulty; either (1st) to say, that our sins are really forgiven before we believe.—Or, (2d) that although they are not, yet according to the tenor of the Covenant of Grace, they shall be, if we do but believe that they are.—Or, (3d) a belief that " my sins are forgiven," must be left out of the definition of justifying faith.—The first was the solution of Antinomians in former ages. But it is so contrary to the express declaration of Scripture (Joh. iii. 18.) that it will not do. The third gives up the whole scheme they contend for.—And so that will not do. The second, which Mr. Marshal has taken, bad as it is, is the only one that is left. Now if they all mean as he does, it is to be wished, they would all speak as plain, that we may precisely know what they intend. This would soon bring the controversy to an issue. But when I read their books, they seem to me sometimes to solve the difficulty one way, and sometimes another. Sometimes they represent as tho' " Pardon was mine absolutely before Faith:" and sometimes just the contrary. Sometimes they say, " We have the clearest evidence from Scripture for this belief:" and sometimes they say, " We have no evidence from Scripture, sense, or reason." Sometimes faith is raised up to " a persuasion that I in particular am pardoned, and shall certainly have eternal life." And then again it sinks down into a mere " belief that I have a common interest in Gospel-offers, such as even reprobates have."*

Paul. Thus, my dear Theron, you may see a little by these Queries, what I think of this kind of Faith.—But there is one most mysterious thing, I desire you to explain. —Not why you doubt—I do not wonder, you are often assaulted with doubts. Nor do I wonder, your friend Aspasio meets with the same conflict.(1) You are, both, men of too much sense and reason, not to feel yourselves a little shocked sometimes, in spite of all your principles.—But this I wonder at—I am surprised, how you ever came to believe. Pray, be so kind, as to give me a particular narrative, how faith was wrought in your heart.

Ther. I had lately made a visit at Philenor's, with my dear Aspasio; where, in the kindest and and most affectionate manner, I was urged to believe; assured, it was my duty and interest, and that God's promise and oath were engaged, that I should never be made ashamed; but it should be according to my faith. And all the precious promises, and gracious invitations in God's Holy Word, were set in order before me, in the most moving language, and I was argued out of all my objections.—Whereupon, after my return home, as I was walking in my garden, longing to have an interest in Christ, meditating on the promises, striving to take them home to myself, praying for the Spirit to witness with my Spirit, that I was a child of God, thus earnestly endeavouring to work up myself to this assurance, and thus waiting for the Holy Spirit;—as I was thinking on the dying love of Christ, those words

And this is all I am to believe. But in a few pages, Faith is raised up again as high as ever.—So, that one knows not where to find them—they seem to be pinched; and not to know how to get out. Therefore, they now run here, and then run there; but know not what to do, to avoid the glaring inconsistence of their scheme: and yet dread to give it up.

At present, for ought that appears, Mr. Marshal's solution is the best that the case can admit of—To be sure Mr. Hervey thinks it the best; as he esteems Mr. Marshal's mystery next to the Bible. And in his preface to Mr. Marshal's book, he says, " I shall rejoice in the prospect of having the Gospel-mystery of Sanctification, stand as a fourth volume to Theron and Aspasio."—And therefore I have a just warrant in the present controversy, to consider it as such. And to view all four volumes as containing one compleat scheme. (1) D. *p.* 353.

seemed to be spoken to me, *O thou of little faith, wherefore dost thou doubt?* Wherefore dost thou doubt of my love to thee, for whom I have shed my blood?—I believed—I was full of love and joy—and for several days, all my thoughts were taken up about Heavenly things. I was weaned from the world. All old things seemed to be passed away, and all things to become new.

Paul. Let any Chriftlefs, gracelefs finner, in your circumftances, believe, as you believed; and from principles which are natural to mankind, he would feel as you felt. And, as all your affections might flow from natural principles, they were no evidence of a fupernatural change; as you may fee proved at large, in a book I have as good an opinion of, as your Afpafio has of Mr. Marfhal's myftery, &c.(1) Therefore, from thefe effects of your faith, you cannot argue, it was no delufion. Becaufe, if it had been a delufion, it might have produced juft the fame.—You will fuffer me therefore to enquire, *What warrant had you for this belief?*—For although *all the promifes of God are* IN CHRIST, *Yea, and Amen,* (2 Cor. i. 20.) yet, to him that is *out of Chrift, God is a confuming fire.* He is *condemned, and the wrath of God abideth on him.* (Joh. iii. 18, 36.)— Pray tell me, muft not a finner be in Chrift, before he is entitled to the promifes?

Ther. Yes—For it is his union with, and relation to Chrift, which lays the foundation for his intereft in all the bleffings purchafed by him. Firft, we are *children,* and then *heirs.* (Rom. viii. 17.) Firft, we are ingrafted into Chrift, *the true vine,* and then partake of the fap. (Joh. xv. 1, 7.) Firft, we are married to Chrift, and then we are interefted in all his riches and glory.(2)

Paul. A charming truth this, my Theron! And if you will attend to it, and be confiftent with yourfelf it muft lead you back from the paths of error, to the high road which goes directly to the Heavenly Zion.—For, if we muft be *in* Chrift, before we are interefted in his benefits; we muft *know* that we are in Chrift, before we can know our interefts in his benefits. And, therefore, the firft direct

(1) *Mr. Edwards on Religious Affections.*
(2) *See all this finely reprefented, as well as rightly ftated,* D *p.* 213, 218. *Whether in a confiftence with the reft of his fcheme, we fhall fee hereafter.*

act of faith cannot confist in believing that his benefits are mine.—Arietta was first married to Philenor, before her debts devolved on him, and all his dignity was derived to her. Had she been carried away with a fond dream, with a full perfuasion, that Philenor, and all his riches and honour were her's, before marriage, and to the neglect of matrimonial rites, she might have enjoyed the comfort of her dream; but must have really lived in widowhood, and died in debt, never the better for the " wealthy and illustrious Philenor." As this is your Afpasio's own simile, I hope you will the more diligently attend to it.(1) Justifying faith is that act, whereby we, being *dead to the law, are married to Christ*. (Rom. vii. 4. 2 Cor. xi. 2) And after marriage we may justly say, *My beloved is mine, and I am his* (Cant. ii. 16.) but not *before*. (Eph. ii. 12. Joh. iii. 18.)

Ther. Yes. Let me tell you, that any Cariftlefs, gracelefs finner in the world, has equal right, with the best saint, to adopt this language, and say, *My beloved is mine, and I am his.* For this ties the very knot,—this constitutes the union (2)

Paul. I think, for once, my Theron, your dear Afpasio himself feems to contradict you. You doubtless remember his words : " *My beloved is mine and I am his*—I dare not say, is the poesy of the mystic ring—but it is the undoubted effect of this divine union."(3)

Ther. Sure I am, my dear Afpasio taught me by the first direct act of faith, to go to God, and say, " Pardon is mine, grace is mine, Christ and all his spiritual blessings are mine :" Not because I am conscious of sanctifying operations in my own breast, but previous to any reflection on inherent graces. I am not therefore, first, by reflection, to know, that I am married to Christ, before I call him my own.— Yea, rather, I must first know, that he is mine, before I can,—before I dare, come to him. This, I am sure, is my Afpasio's doctrine.(4)

Paul. But then Christ and all his spiritual blessings are your's, before you are in Christ ; which is contrary to what Afpasio admits (5) And contrary to the plain sense of the New Testament, as you but just now stated the matter yourself.—But to dwell upon this inconsistence no longer,—

(1) D. *p.* 215. (2) D *p.* 343, 344. (3) D. *p.* 218.
(4) D. *p.* 312, 313, 358, 302. (5) D. *p.* 213, 218.

Pray, tell me what warrant you had from Scripture, to believe, that Chrift and all his fpiritual bleffings were your's.

Ther. I was awakened to fome fenfe of my danger of eternal ruin, I longed to believe that my fins were pardoned, and that Chrift was mine; but I could not fee my title clear. Afpafio told me, it was "perfectly clear." That I had as good a warrant for this belief, as a neighbouring clergyman had to take any book in my library, whom I had lately affured, "that he was as welcome to any book as though they were all his own." Yea, as good a warrant for this belief, as one of my fervants had to believe me, when I gave him a farm for his own. (1)

Paul. Shocking!—I would not treat an awakened finner fo, for all the world.—But how did Afpafio make it out, that your title to pardon was thus clear, when Mr. Marfhal, his favourite author owns, there is no evidence of the thing from Scripture, fenfe, or reafon?

Ther. He referred me to Joh. vii. 37. *If any man thirft, let him come unto me and drink.* But you thirft, faid he; therefore to you, this promife is made. (2) And he was always encouraging me to this belief, by taking a kind notice of my earneft prayers, forrows, tears, good defires, and fenfe of unworthinefs. (3) And from this quarter my firft encouragement arofe to hope and believe, that Chrift, pardon, grace and glory were mine.

Paul. But according to this, O my Theron, your own awakenings, earneft prayers, forrows, tears, good defires, and fenfe of unworthinefs, laid the firft foundation of your faith. This was the fecret language of your heart, "To fuch a one as I am, the promifes belong: and fo I may fafely believe, they are all my own."—As much your own as your fervant's little farm was his. And if your encouragement to believe, took its rife from your own inherent qualifications; if your own goodnefs, in whatever humble form, emboldened you to come to Chrift; your hope of acceptance was really bottomed on your own righteoufnefs: and fo your's is a felf-righteous faith. And if this be the cafe, a clear fight of the badnefs of your heart, and of the ftrictnefs of the law, would entirely kill your faith. (Rom. vii 9)

(1) D. *p.* 269, 273. (2) D. *p.* 270. (3) D *p.* 157, 158, 207, 208, 220, 265, 266, 289, 290, 293, 294.

If your good defires, like fo much money in hand, encouraged you to come to Chrift; your courage would fail you, did you know, that the beft defires you ever had, according to Law and ftrict Juftice, merit eternal damnation. Did you thus feel yourfelf without money, you would not dare to come.

Ther. But is it not true? Are not the promifes made to thofe that *thirft*? Joh. vii. 37. That *labour and are heavy laden?* Mat. xi. 28, &c.

Paul. Thefe are not promifes, my Theron, which convey a title to pardon and falvation to Sinners out of Chrift, on condition of their good defires. They are rather invitations to a union with Chrift by a true and living faith. They give a Sinner a good warrant to come to Chrift: to come *without money and without price* (Ifai. lv. 1.) and thofe who thus come, fhall find reft to their fouls. But they give no grounds to one out of Chrift, encouraged by his own righteoufnefs to believe that pardon, grace, and glory, are his.

Ther. I did not mean that my own good defires, prayers, &c. gave me a right to believe. I had a good right before. As an "abandoned Sinner," (1) I had an actual right to Chrift and all his benefits, by an "Actual gift from the Almighty Majefty," juft as my fervant had to his little farm, by my donation. (2)

Paul. After you had given the little farm to your fervant, it was his. It was his, before he believed it his.—Your donation made it his, and not his belief. It was his before he believed it, and whether he believed it, or not. He had fufficient evidence to believe it his, previous to his belief. Now if Chrift and all his benefits are your's in this fenfe, then you was juftified, adopted, fanctified, and entitled to eternal glory, while fecure in fin; months, nay, years, before any of your converfation with Afpafio.—Yea, your title is as old as the Gofpel. Which you confider as your deed of gift, or as Chrift's laft Will and Teftament, in which all thefe legacies were bequeathed to you. Your title, your abfolute title commenced at the death of the Teftator.—" When your old acquaintance Charicles, left you a handfome legacy, what did you do to eftablifh your title, and make it your own?"

(1) *D. p.* 307, 308. (2) *D. p.* 272, 273.

Ther. "My title was pre-established, by my friend's donation. I had nothing to do, but to claim, to accept, and to possess." And I did the very same in the present case. (1) And ever since this first act of Faith, "On this unalterable ground, I assert and maintain my title. Pardon is mine, Grace is mine, Christ, and all his Spiritual blessings are mine; because all these precious privileges are consigned over to me in the everlasting 'Gospel." (2) 'This is the proper notion of believing.—" When I sent a message to my tenant, assuring him, I had cancelled the bond, and forgiven his debt; he believed the message to be true.—So I give credit to the gracious declarations of my God.—So I believe." (3)

(1) *D. p.* 255. (2) *D. p.* 362.
(3) *D. p.* 297, 298.---*And with Theron agrees Mr. Boston, who in his book on the two Covenants, maintains, that Christ in his last Will and Testament, did actually bequeath regenerating Grace, Justification, Adoption, Sanctification, and Eternal Life, freely, absolutely and unconditionally, to every Sinner of Adam's race. And adds, that Christ himself is also executor of this will, and by his office as such obliged to make out all these legacies to all the legatees, that are pleased to put in their claim, and make their demands. And faith, according to him, consists in believing all is mine, and in claiming and taking possession of all as my own. (See p.* 114, 199, 214.) *And arises from no higher principle than self-preservation.* (P. 262, 263.)
Saint Paul used to say, If children, then heirs. *(Rom. viii.* 17. *Gal. iii.* 29.) But according to this new gospel, it is, if Sinners, then heirs. And this will be reckoned good news for unregenerate Sinners. They are no longer at God's sovereign mercy, according to Rom. ix. 15. Nor need they come as poor beggars, according to Luke xviii. 13. Their title to all things "Is perfectly clear," even while unregenerate and out of Christ. And they may come as heirs, who have a legal right to make demands; and put in their claim, and say "Pardon is mine, I claim it, I demand it as my own." And the executer is obliged to answer their demands, and give out their legacies. *This scheme, were it true, would suit corrupt nature, even better than the Arminian. As we all had rather have estates left to us by wills, than be at pains to work for them: So it is easier to claim and demand Heaven, than*

Paul. To whom are Christ, pardon, grace and glory, consigned over and conveyed in the Gospel-grant? What are their names? Or what are their characters? Who are the men so highly favoured? In wills and in deeds of gift, you know, the parties, to whom any thing is bequeathed, or given, are mentioned by name. Is it so in the Gospel-grant? Are all these blessings entailed on believers, or on sinners, as such?

Ther. On Sinners, on all Sinners of Adam's race; and that considered merely as Sinners: as my dear Aspasio proved at large. (1) And that which is thus freely given to every Sinner, any Sinner in particular has a good warrant to look upon as his own. Thus, then, stands my warrant to believe. All these blessings are given to Sinners, as such:— But I am a Sinner: Therefore, all these blessings are given to me. (2)

Paul. That is, "all Sinners are justified, adopted, sanctified, and entitled to eternal life: But I am a Sinner:

to do as the Pharisee did in Luk. xviii. 12. Those texts in Heb. viii. 10, 11, 12, and ix. 15, 16, 17, on which they pretend to found their scheme, are plainly nothing to the purpose. For God does not say, " This is the Covenant I will make with all the sinful race of Adam ; I will write my Law in their hearts, &c." But God says, " This is the Covenant I will make with the House of Israel." But he is not a Jew, who is one outwardly. Rom. ii, 28 29. The children of the promise are counted for the seed. Rom. ix. 8. If ye be Christ's, then are ye Abraham's seed, and heirs according to the Promise. Gal. iii. 29. But if out of Christ, we are condemned, and the wrath of God abideth on us. Joh. iii. 18. 36. And we can claim nothing. No, not another moment of time, nor liberty to breathe another breath in God's world. We have a title to not one minute's forbearance ; But God may send us to Hell this instant. Rom. iii. 19. Gal. iii. 10.---Object. But it is said to the elder brother, All that I have is thine. Luk. xv. 31.—Ans. Yes. And with design to describe the temper of a Pharisee's heart. The younger son represented Publicans and Sinners, and the elder the Pharisees. (See ver. 1, 2.) The poor Publican thought he had no claim to make, but lay at mercy. Luk. xviii. 13. The Pharisees said in their hearts, all is our own.

(1) D. p. 298, 319. (2) D. p. 305.

Therefore I am justified, adopted, sanctified, and entitled to eternal life." But my dear Theron, if you know what you say, if you really mean as you say, and if you affirm these sentiments are "Strictly conformable to the unerring Oracles" of God, then, all Adam's race are, according to you, actually justified, adopted, sanctified, and entitled to eternal glory. And thus your devout Aspasio carries matters farther than even the famous Doctor John Taylor, whose key to the Apostolic writings is not half so heterodox as this; how much soever condemned by all the friends of vital piety. For he only supposes, that all within the visible church, are justified, adopted, &c. and not all Adam's race.

Besides, how is all this consistent with the words you just now cited out of Mr. Marshal's Mystery, a book your Aspasio values next to the Bible? "We have no absolute promise or declaration in Scripture, that God certainly will or doth give Christ and his salvation to any one of us in particular; neither do we know it to be true already, by scripture, sense or reason, before we assure ourselves absolutely of it: Yea, we are without Christ's salvation at present, in a state of sin and misery, under the curse and wrath of God. This is a strange kind of assurance.—— Therefore, no wonder if it be found weak and imperfect, and difficult to be obtained, and assaulted with many doubtings. We are constrained to believe other things on the clear evidence we have, that they are true, whether we believe them or no; so that we cannot deny our assent, without rebelling against the light of our senses, reason, or conscience. But here our assurance is not impressed on our thoughts by any evidence of the thing; but we must work it out in ourselves, by the assistance of the Spirit of GOD."

Yea, how is all this consistent with your own experience and with the experience of your Aspasio? For if all spiritual blessings are by a deed of gift absolutely made over to all Sinners of Adam's race, and that considered merely as such, plainly in the Gospel, so that their "Title is perfectly clear;" then as true as the Gospel is true, all are absolutely entitled to pardon, grace and glory, before they believe, and whether they believe or not. And I never hear of you, or your friend doubting the truth of the Gospel itself. How then can you have any doubts about your title to Heaven? Why was you so backward to believe your title? Or why was your friend so ready to "Feel for you, and sympathize with you?" How could it be so difficult to believe, while at the same time he "Beheld his title perfectly clear?" (1) Did ever any mortal act thus as to temporal things? Was ever a son of Adam put to great difficulty to believe an inheritance to be his own, when he saw with his own eyes, "his title was perfectly clear," and had the deed of gift well executed in his own hands? My dear Theron, I am even tempted to doubt, whether you, yourselves believe your own scheme. Yea, it seems plain, you are all the while afraid you are deluded. And no wonder, says Mr. Marshal, for you have no evidence from Scripture, sense or reason.—Pray, did your Aspasio ever attempt to prove his scheme out of the Bible?

Ther. Yes. And once speaking of his differing from the orthodox, I remember he said, "I dare not purchase their approbation, I dare not attempt a coalition of sentiments. Pray my dear friend, said he to me, what is the standard of orthodoxy? Is it the word of Revelation? This speaks once, yea twice, nay, some hundreds of times in our favour." (2) And first and last, I am apt to think, he mentioned above an hundred texts of Scripture, to prove his point.

Paul, Out of this great number, pray select some of the most plain and full to the purpose; and on which he seemed to lay the greatest stress; and let us carefully examine them.

Ther. There are many texts which teach us, that God has given his son to a lost world. Isai. ix. 6. *To us a son is given.* (3) Joh. iii. 16. *God so loved the world, that he gave his only begotten son.* (4) Other texts declare as follows. Isai. liii. 6. *God laid on him the iniquity of us all.* (5) 1 Tim. i. 15. *He came into the world to save Sinners.* 1 Pet. iii. 18. *Died for the unjust.* (6) 1 Cor. xv. i. *Christ died for our sins.* (7) 1 Joh. v. 9. *This is the record that God hath given to us eternal life.* (8) Act. xiii. 38. *To you is preached the remission of sins.* Act. ii. 39. *The*

(1) D. p. 269, 353. (2) D. p. 335. (3) D. p. 308.
(4) D. p. 305. (5) D. p. 304. (6) D. p. 299. (7) D.
p. 319. (8) D. p. 319.

promise is to you, and to all that are afar off, even as many as the Lord our God shall call. (1) In which Scriptures, you see, Christ and all his spiritual blessings are given and made over to Sinners, as such, freely and absolutely: So as that every one has a good warrant to believe they are his own. And if we would give the same credit to God as my Tenant did to me, we need not, we could not doubt, but that they are all our own. (2)

"When Jonah, in pursuance of the Divine command, cried and said, *Yet forty days and Nineveh shall be overthrown,*" without mentioning any by name, "*All, from the least even unto the greatest, believed;*" applied the threatning to themselves. When Moses speaking of the Manna, said, "*This is the bread which the Lord hath given you to eat,*" without mentioning any by name; the whole congregation supposed, they had all and every one a good right to take and eat. So when our Saviour says, "*My Father giveth you the true bread from Heaven.*" *(*Joh. vi. 32.) Alluding to the Manna, we may all and every one believe it is our own. (3)

Paul. Your Aspasio always supposes, that all the blessings of the Gospel are granted absolutely and without any condition; so that we have nothing to do, but to believe they are all our own. Whereas, there is always a condition expressed or implied. For according to the constant tenor of the Gospel, we must first be in Christ, by a true and living faith, before the blessings of the Gospel are our's. (4)—To descend to particulars.—

(1) *D. p.* 303.   (2) *D. p.* 298.   (3) *D. p.* 305, 307.
(4) *All writers on this scheme maintain, that pardon, grace and glory, are unconditionally and absolutely given, granted and made over to all Sinners of Adam's race. And this absolute Grant gives each of us a good warrant to believe "pardon, grace and glory are mine."—Reader stop, and think one minute—If the grant is not absolute, it does not make pardon mine, nor give me a right to believe it mine—If it is absolute, it makes pardon mine before I believe it; and so I am justified before Faith.—"No, say they, it is not mine before I believe it mine. But if I believe it mine, it is mine." But one would think, if it is not mine before I believe, I believe a lie. My sins are pardoned before I believe, or they are not. If they are pardoned before Faith, then I am*

It is true, God so loved the world as to give his only begotten Son. For what? To die for us. To what end? *That whosoever believeth in him, should not perish, but have everlasting life.* He that is united to Christ by Faith, therefore, shall be saved. But those who are out of Christ have no interest in his salvation; but are under a present condemnation.—Condemned already. And the wrath of God abideth on them. " Pardon is mine."—No—Condemned already. " God is reconciled to me." No.— *The wrath of God abideth on me.* Joh. iii. 16, 18, 36.

It is true, This is the record that God hath given to us eternal life. But this life is in his Son. Therefore, he that is by Faith united to Christ, hath eternal life. For he that hath the Son, hath life. But those who are out of Christ, have no interest in this eternal life. *For he that hath not the Son, hath not life.* 1 Joh. v. 11, 12.

It is true, That through this man, is preached unto you the forgiveness of sins. But who hath an interest in this forgiveness? Who is that blessed man that is justified? Those who are out of Christ? No. But, *By him all that believe, are justified,* Act. xiii. 38, 39.

Again, it is true, The promise is to you. And what then? Repent and be baptized every one of you in the name of Jesus Christ, for the Remission of sins. Were their sins already forgiven? No. Repent and be converted that your sins may; not because they are, but that they may *be blotted out.* Act. ii. 38, 39, and iii. 19.—

not justified by Faith, but before Faith. If they are not, then I believe a lie.—" No, says Mr. Marshal, *according to thy Faith, it shall be unto thee.*" i. e. *If* " *without any evidence from Scripture, sense or reason,*" *I believe that to be true, which is not true, it shall become true. This is the heart and soul of their scheme.*—Keep this in constant view, suffer no ambiguous words to drown your mind; and it is easy to see, that there is not one text in the Bible to their purpose. Yea, they give us an exact definition of delusion, which properly consists in this, viz. " *I believe something to be true, which is not true, till in my imagination it seems true; and so I take the comfort of it, as though it were true.*" Whereas, in saving Faith there is no truth believed, but what is plainly revealed in the Gospel; as will appear presently.

But what was their state while impenitent? *Except ye repent, ye shall all likewise perish.* Luk. xiii. 3, 5.

Lastly, it is' true, The whole congregation of Israel were welcome to take the manna and eat. And 'tis true, that all mankind are welcome to receive Christ, the true bread, and eat, and live forever. For this eating is the same as uniting to Christ, by a true and living Faith.— *He that eateth my flesh and drinketh my blood, dwelleth in me, and I in him.* Therefore, *He that eateth me, even he shall live by me.* But what is the state of Sinners out of Christ? Have they eternal life? No. *Except ye eat the flesh of the son of man, and drink his blood, ye have no life in you.* Joh. vi. 32, 57.

Thus the very texts you build your scheme upon, are all against you. What warrant, therefore, has a Sinner out of Christ, to say, " pardon is mine, grace is mine, Christ and all his spiritual blessings are mine?" For these precious privileges are not consigned over to him in the everlasting Gospel, while in such a state. Nor shall he ever have an interest in them, unless he is first united to Christ, by a true and living Faith.

Ther. If the curse of the Law, which is delivered in general terms, not mentioning Theron by name, belongs to Theron; why do not the promises of the Gospel, delivered also in general terms, not mentioning Theron by name, belong to Theron too? (1) The Ninevites, from the least to the greatest, made particular application to themselves.

Paul. The Law curses none but those who have already broken it; and the Gospel pardons none but those who have already complied with it. Theron has already broken the Law, and fallen under the curse: Let Theron comply with the Gospel, and he shall be entitled to the blessing. The curse of the Law was not your's, 'till you broke it: Nor are the blessings of the Gospel your's 'till you comply with it. For it is written, *He that believeth not, is condemned already.* A truth, which all unbelievers, from the least even unto the greatest, should after the example of the Ninevites, make particular application of, to themselves. I must, therefore, still repeat it, what warrant from the word of God have you for your Faith.?

(1) D. p. 306.

Ther. Moses led the whole Congregation of Israel, at the side of the Red-Sea, tho' the greatest part of them were in a graceless state, to call God their God. (Exod. xv. 2.) And to confirm them in this belief, God himself, from Mount Sinai, and generally through all the Law of Moses, says, speaking to the whole Congregation, *I am the Lord, thy God.* (Exod. xx. 2.) And in the days of Jeremiah, when there was scarce a good man to be found among them (Jer. v. 1.) and the generality were devoted to idolatry, and obstinately impenitent; yet, to the whole nation God says, *Turn, O backsliding Children, for I am married unto you.* (Jer. iii. 14.) And he teaches them to say, *We come unto thee, for thou art the Lord our God.* (ver. 22) And invites them to look upon him as their Father. (verse 4.) And as the Jews were all circumcised at eight days old, and so brought into covenant with God, they had all thereby a good warrant to look upon God as their God, and to believe that he was their father, and would save them. The same may be said of all baptized persons in the Christian world. (1)

Paul. If this proves any thing to your purpose, it proves that all the Christless Sinners in Christendom, how wicked soever, although even buried up in Popish idolatry, are, if they are baptized, all of them married to Christ, children of God, and heirs of Heaven. Into what strange absurdities and inconsistences do you run, my dear Theron!

As to circumcision, the Jews in our Saviour's day seemed to think, that it entitled them to salvation. But our Saviour taught them, that notwithstanding their circumcision, they were, while unregenerate, (John iii. 3.) and antecedent to Faith and union with Christ, under condemnation and wrath. (ver. 18, 36.) And Saint Paul affirms, that the Jew as well as Gentile, notwithstanding their circumcision, stood guilty before God, without any title to life, antecedent to their regeneration and union with Christ by a true and living Faith. (Rom. ii. 28, 29, and iii. 1, 2, 9, 19, 28. Gal. iii. 10. 29.) And the same may be said of those who are baptized.

As to the texts of Scripture you refer to, their true sense may be easily seen, if we consider God's covenant with Abraham; in which he promised to be *A God to him and*

(1) M. *p.* 28, 182, 185. D. *p.* 312, 343.

to his seed. (Gen. xvii.) And God's covenant at Mount Sinai, in which he took the whole nation to be his peculiar people. (Exod. xix.) From which he calls himself *The Lord their God.* : And on account of which, he is called their Husband, and they are said to be married to him, and are charged with whoredom and adultery for going after other Gods ; and are invited to return to him, as a wife to her husband, and to call him their God and Father. Not that they had any title to pardon, grace and glory, while *uncircumcised in heart.* (Jer. xxxi. 31, 32. Rom. ii. 28, 29.) With these observations in mind, it will be easy to understand the language used commonly in the Prophets, particularly in Hof. ii. throughout.

Ther. But it is the proper business of Faith, "To appropriate and take home to ourselves the grace of God, which lies in the common indefinite grant of the Gospel." Therefore, as pardon, grace and glory, are, all of them, given and granted to sinners as such ; by Faith, I, a Sinner take home these blessings to myself, i. e. I believe they are mine. (1)

Paul. Yes. But my Theron, there is no such absolute, unconditional grant contained in the Bible. Nor do the Scriptures teach that Faith is of such a nature.

Ther. Yes. But Saint Paul declares that *Faith is the evidence of things not seen* (Heb. xi. 1.) and exhibits a clear demonstration of our right to enjoy them. (2)

Paul. Faith cometh by hearing, and hearing by the word of God. (Rom. x. 17.) If therefore, the word of God gives a sinner, while out of Christ, no absolute unconditional right to the blessings of the Gospel, Faith can see none. Faith cannot see what is not, neither can it believe without evidence. All the believers in Saint Paul's catalogue, had good evidence for what they believed. But you have no evidence from "Scripture, sense or reason" for what you believe ; as you, yourself are obliged to own.

Ther. But all those figurative descriptions of Faith, which occur in holy writ, imply this appropriating belief. (3)

Paul. No, my dear Theron, not one of them. Is Christ viewed in the beginning of Saint John's Gospel, as the Creator of all things, who, under the Mosaic dispensation, sustained the glorious character of God and King

(1) *D. p.* 305, 314, 317.   (2) *D. p.* 318.   (3) *D. p* 320.

of Israel, now come to tabernacle among men, come to his own people, as the promised Messiah? He is to be acknowledged, received, and honoured according to his character. But he came to his own, and his own received him not: Did not own him for the Messiah, nor believe in, nor honour him as such. Although he was indeed the very God and King of Israel, who of old dwelt in their Tabernacle and Temple in the form of God, now come to tabernacle in flesh, in the form of a servant: Yet they rejected him, called him a deceiver, and crucified him for claiming to be the Son of God and King of the Jews.— But to as many as received him as the promised Messiah, with all their hearts, gave he power to become the son of God, even to as many as believed in his name. Not, that believed their sins were pardoned without any evidence from Scripture, sense, or reason, but that believed in his name—Trusted in his mediation, merits and atonement, that through his name they might obtain forgiveness of sins and eternal life. (Joh. i.1, 12.) Is Christ compared to the brazen serpent? We are not to believe that we are healed; but to look to him for healing.—Is he compared to a bridegroom? We are not to believe he is our husband;— but as chaste virgins to be espoused to him, that by this spiritual marriage he may become our husband.—Is he compared to the city of refuge? We are not to believe ourselves safe; but to fly to him for safety.—Is he compared to bread and water? We are not to believe our hunger and thirst are assuaged; but to eat the living bread, and drink the living water, that they may be so.—In a word, is he the great High-priest, who has entered into Heaven with the blood of atonement in his hand, by and through whom we may come to God for all things, in full assurance of acceptance in his name? We are not to believe that pardon, grace, and glory are our's; but to draw nigh to God through him, that of God's infinite grace through him, we may be pardoned, sanctified and saved.

Ther. But David, Job, Habakkuk, Paul, the Council at Jerusalem, yea, all the Saints in Scripture, use this appropriating language. They all speak the language of assurance. (1)

Paul. And good reason why, for they all knew, they

---

(1) D. p: 325, 327.

were sincere godly men, from a consciousness to their own inherent graces. But there is not a Saint to be found in the Bible, that believes pardon, grace and glory to be his own, without any evidence from "Scripture, sense or reason." Forgive me, Sir, if I should say, this kind of Faith the Bible is as great a stranger to, as to the doctrine of purgatory.

Ther. "I know no other justifying Faith, but that which relates to the Gospel, and believes its report. But here, I find, lies the core and root of our controversy. This is the precise point to be settled; what it is to believe." (1)

Paul. No, no, my dear Theron, "The core and root of the controversy" lies not here. You ought to believe the report of the Gospel," and all the truths of the Gospel, with a full assurance; yea, with all the full assurance of Faith. But Protestant writers, for above these hundred years, have been testifying against your kind of Faith, because the thing believed is not contained in the Gospel.—The Gospel makes no such report. But the thing believed is a lie.—Here my friend, here lies "The core and root of the controversy," as Mr. Marshal well knew. (2) And it is a little strange, that your Aspasio should not know it too. However, pray tell me what you mean, by believing the report of the Gospel.

Ther. "The Lord declares by his prophet, *I, even I am he, that blotteth out thy transgressions.* To believe, is to subscribe this declaration: To subscribe it with our hand, and profess with our heart, *Lord, it is done, as thou hast said.*" My transgressions are blotted out. (3)

Paul. But my dear Theron, this declaration was made above two thousand years ago. Do you date your justification so far back? Or do you think the words have had any new meaning put to them by God, of late; which two thousand years ago they did not mean?

Ther. No. I appropriate and take home the blessing to myself: And so believe the report of the Gospel.

Paul. This is not to believe what the Gospel reports; but rather to make a new Gospel. This is not to believe the truths already revealed; but to make a new Revelation. That the transgressions of Theron, a Christless Sinner, are blotted out, is not taught in this text, nor in any text

(1) *D. p.* 328. (2) *M. p.* 166. (3) *D. p.* 329.

in all the sacred volume, as you yourself very well know. And if this be what you mean by an appropriating Faith, then Mr. Marshall's account of it is very just: it is a believing without any evidence, from "Scripture, sense or reason.(1)"

(1) *The whole party maintain, with Wendelinus, that in the first direct act of Faith, I believe " my sins are forgiven."— And the whole party assert, that before I believed it, " my sins were not forgiven." Therefore, the whole party must concede with Mr. Marshall, that the thing I believe, " was not true before I believed it." And consequently, that I do believe it " without any evidence from Scripture, sense or reason." For if it was not true, there could be no evidence of its truth. And yet the whole party pretend to ground their belief upon Scripture. So that this is the strangest scheme of religion in this respect, that ever was advanced in the Christian world.—The thing I believe as true, is not true before I believe it; and yet I believe it because it is true! It is not contained in Scripture; yet I believe it, because it is contained in Scripture! I know it is no part of the Gospel-revelation; yet I venture my soul upon it for eternity, as the very Gospel of Christ! Now, how do these men feel satisfied in themselves, in believing such inconsistencies? Why thus—" The Gospel makes an absolute unconditional grant of pardon and salvation to all the sinful race of Adam: But I am a Sinner of Adam's race; therefore, pardon and salvation are mine."—But then, one would think they were mine before I believed it, and whether I believed it or no. If the grant doth not make them mine, why do I believe they are mine? If the grant does make them mine, then they are mine before I believe: And so we are not justified by Faith, but* BEFORE *Faith, contrary to the whole tenor of Scripture. No, say some, " I have by grant a common but not a saving interest." But the thing granted is " salvation: and the grant is absolute:—Therefore, " I shall be saved." I ought to believe, that " I shall be saved;" Yea, they say, I make God a liar, if I do not; but surely, if I believe I shall be saved, I believe I have a saving interest. And so, I believe I have by the grant, what I know is not contained in the grant: and so believe, " without any evidence from Scripture, sense or reason." And yet I ground my belief wholly upon Scripture.—They say, " The grant makes it mine, so as to give me a right to believe it mine, and claim it, and possess it as mine." But then, I ought to believe it mine, precisely in the same* SENSE.

G

Ther. But Christ has expresssly promised, that *according to my Faith, so shall it be to me.* Matth. ix. 29.(1)

Paul. Believe ye, that I am able to do this? said Christ to the two blind men, who cried, *Thou Son of David, have mercy on us.*—They said unto him, *Yea, Lord.* To be sure, they had sufficient evidence to believe it, from the miracles he had already wrought. On which our Saviour touched their eyes: saying, *According to your Faith, be it unto you.*

in which the grant makes it mine. Thus, if the grant makes it mine as being a child of Adam; then I ought to believe it mine, as knowing I am a child of Adam.—If the grant makes it mine, only as being in Christ; then I ought to believe it mine, only as knowing that I am in Christ.—If the grant only makes a common interest mine; then I ought to believe a common interest only to be mine.—If the grant makes a saving interest mine; then I ought to believe a saving interest mine. And what is mine by grant, if the grant is absolute, is mine before I believe it, and whether I believe it, or not. No, say they, "It is not mine before I believe; and yet I must believe it mine. I have no evidence from Scripture; and yet my Faith is wholly founded on Scripture. The Scripture says no such thing any where; and yet the Scripture plainly says this being in hundreds of places. My sins are not forgiven; and yet I make God a liar, *if I do not believe they are forgiven. It is not true, as yet, nor do I know it ever will be true; but I must believe it, without any evidence from Scripture, sense or reason: And in so doing, I believe the report of the Gospel; although the Gospel never made such a report." If I can believe all these contradictions with all my heart, I am a true believer, and shall be saved. If not, I am blind, carnal, legal; and finally must suffer the pains of eternal damnation for my unbelief.—The Infidels of the age (and no wonder infidelity prevails) stand by; hear the dispute; shake their sides:—The Devil says, "So I would have it." The Daughter of Zion puts on sackcloth, looks up to Heaven, and cries, "Hast thou forsaken the Earth, O Lord! When wilt thou return and scatter these clouds; and cause light to break out, spread and prevail; and darkness and error to flee away! O when shall that blessed day come, that the* knowledge of the Lord shall fill the Earth, as the waters cover the Sea! *When shall* Satan be bound, that he may deceive the nations no more!"

(1) M. p. 247.

And what, my Theron, is this to your purpose? who have no evidence from Scripture, sense or reason, for what you believe. Our Saviour never told Sinners, that if they would believe pardon, grace and glory were theirs, it should be unto them according to their Faith: but frequently taught, that many who believed so, would finally be disappointed. Matth. vii. 21, 27.—Luke xiii. 24, 30.

Ther. Yes, our Saviour expressly said, *What things soever ye desire when ye pray, believe that ye receive them, and ye shall have them.* Mark xi. 24. (1)

Paul. Our Saviour had cursed the barren fig-tree, and it was dried up from the roots. At which his disciples wondering, our Saviour told them, that whenever they were called to perform any miraculous works, and were looking up to God to do them, they must firmly believe he would do the thing, how great soever it was, even although as difficult as to *remove a mountain and cast it into the sea.* And it is plain, they had sufficient evidence, for such a belief: as they knew that God Almighty stood engaged to effect the miraculous works, which he had commissioned them to declare, should be done. Mark, xi. 20, 24.

Ther. But the Apostle James directs all Christians, even when praying for divine wisdom and grace, to *ask in Faith, nothing wavering.* Jam. i. 6. (2)

Paul. To ask in Faith—In the Faith of what? Of truths revealed in the Gospel, concerning the way of our access to God in the name of Christ, our great high Priest, and God's readiness to hear and answer all requests, agreeable to his Will, put up unto him in his Name. These truths ought to be, these truths must be firmly believed. But in order to our going to God in full assurance of Faith, there is no need, I hope, that we believe as true, things, the truth of which we have no evidence of, "from Scripture, sense, or reason." Read the second chapter of this epistle, and you may see the Apostle James was no friend to a presumptuous Faith, a Faith built on no evidence.

Ther. But I am invited in the most affectionate manner, to believe that Christ loves me and will save me, in 2 Cor. v. 20. "*As though God did beseech you by us, we pray you in Christ's stead, be ye reconciled to God.* Hark! 'tis the voice

(1) M. *p.* 174.   (2) D. *p.* 342.

of infinitely condescending love, speaking by his ambassador—Sinners accept my great salvation. Enjoy what I have purchased for you by my dying agonies. Do not suspect my kindness, or refuse my gifts. This will wound me deeper than the spear which pierced my side.—O the grace of our exalted King!—After all this, can I entertain the least doubt, whether I have a permission to believe firmly?(1) Did the judge ever beseech a condemned criminal to accept of pardon? Does the creditor beseech a ruined debtor, to receive an acquittance in full? Yet our Almighty Lord, and our Eternal judge, not only vouchsafes to offer these blessings, but invites us—intreats us—with the most tender and repeated importunity solicits us, not to reject them." (2)

Paul. In these words you are invited to be reconciled to God; and not to believe that God is reconciled to you.—You may be even ravished, to think of the one, but still be so inattentive to the other, as not to take any notice of it, although before you, in one of the most remarkable texts in the Bible.

Ther. But we are strictly commanded by God himself, to believe on the name of his Son Jesus Christ (1 Joh. iii. 23.) and have God's promise and oath to assure us, we shall certainly be saved, if we do. (3)

Paul. True. Yet Christ has never taught us, that Faith consists in believing, that " pardon is mine, grace is mine, Christ and all his spiritual blessings are mine." But has given us the strongest assurance, that many who are very confident of their title to Heaven, shall finally go to Hell.—Matth. vii. 22.

Ther. Yes, Sir. Suffer me in my turn, to put on the airs of assurance, and to affirm, that this is that very notion of Faith, which was taught, and which was approved as genuine, by our blessed Saviour.—For, " our Lord bears this testimony concerning Thomas; *Thomas thou hast believed.* Now then, I think, we have got an infallible touchstone. Let us examine what that is, which Jesus Christ calls believing. Whatever it be, it is the determination of Truth itself; and should pass for a verdict, from which there lies no appeal. And this, this is the confession of Thomas, *my*

(1) D. *p.* 350. (2) D. *Edit. I. vol.* 1. *p.* 132.
(3) D. *p.* 350, 353.

LORD, and *my* GOD! This, this expresses what our divine Master calls *believing*. When, therefore, we confess with our lips, and are persuaded in our hearts, that Jesus is our Lord, who bought us with his blood; that Jesus is our God, who will exert all his adorable perfections for our good; then we truly believe. We believe in our Saviour's sense of the Word; we have that Faith, which he allows to be genuine." (1)

Paul. Pray, my dear Theron, as your all lies at stake, your all for eternity, do take the bible, and read the whole paragraph, with the heart of an honest man.

Ther. I will.—Heaven forbid I should act a dishonest part in an affair of such infinite importance! Joh. xx. 24. *But Thomas, one of the twelve, was not with them when Jesus came, ver.* 25, *The other disciples therefore said unto him, "We have seen the Lord." But he said unto them, "Except I shall see in his hands the print of the nails, and put my finger into the print of the nails, and thrust my hand into his side, I will not believe," ver.* 26. *And after eight days, again his disciples were within, and Thomas with them. Then came Jesus, the doors being shut, and stood in the midst, and said, "Peace be unto you," ver.* 27. *Then said he to Thomas, "reach hither thy finger, and behold my hands; and reach hither thy hand, and thrust it into my side: and be not faithless, but believing," ver.* 28. *And Thomas answered, and said unto him " My Lord, and my God," ver.* 29. *Jesus said unto him, " Thomas, because thou hast seen me, thou hast believed: blessed are they that have not seen, and yet have believed.*

Paul. No comment is needed. It is impossible the sense of the words can be made plainer. The thing that Thomas was so faithless about, was not his particular interest in Christ; nor was this the thing he believed, that Christ died for him in particular. But the resurrection of Christ was the thing, the only thing, in question with him. Overjoyed to see him, feel him, hear him, know him, in the language of fervent love, ready to clasp him in his arms, he cries out, *my Lord, and my God!* Thus then stands the argument.—Because Thomas believed that Christ was risen from the dead, on the clearest evidence; therefore justifying Faith consists in believing, that " pardon is mine, grace is mine, Christ and all his spiritual blessings are mine," without any evidence at all, from " Scripture, sense, or reason." My

(1) D. *p.* 229, 230.

dear Theron, was ever book abused and perverted in this apostate world, one half so much, as is the holy Bible!

Ther. But is it not true with relation to every sinner, and so with relation to me, that "Christ has bought me with his blood, and will exert all his adorable perfections for my good?"

Paul. Must I again put you in mind of what your favourite author so plainly affirms? "We have no absolute promise or declaration in Scripture, that God certainly will or doth give Christ and his salvation to any one of us in particular; neither do we know it to be true already, by Scripture, sense, or reason, before we assure ourselves of it. Our assurance is not impressed by any evidence of the thing; but we must work it out in ourselves by the assistance of the spirit of God." And that your Aspasio not only likes the book in general, but heartily approves of this passage in particular, you may be assured, from the notice he has taken of it, in his preface to Mr. Marshall's Mystery.

Ther. Yes, and I approve it too. For I never supposed it was any where taught in Scripture, that "Christ has bought me with his blood, and will exert all his adorable perfections for my good," and so certainly save me in particular. I know there is no such thing affirmed in Scripture. I never pretended there was. And you have misrepresented our scheme, in supposing it follows from what we affirm of the free grant of the Gospel, that we are justified, adopted, and entitled to eternal glory, before we believe. We hold no such thing. There is no such thing revealed in the oracles of truth. And indeed if there was, I should not need any special assistance of the spirit in the work of believing. That I should be saved, would be as plain a truth as any other in the Bible. And did I believe the Scriptures to be true, I could not doubt of this, any more than of any other plain truth therein contained.—Whereas, you know, it is impossible for a man, although he is satisfied the Bible is the word of God, merely by his own strength and reason to bring himself to believe, unless the spirit first witnesses with his spirit, that he is a child of God. Because, before this, we have no evidence of the thing from Scripture, sense, or reason. But when "the divine spirit brings Christ and his righteousness nigh unto us, in the promise of the Gospel; clearing at the same time our right and warrant to intermeddle withall, with out fear of vicious intromiſſion;" then we can appropriate what lies in the general promiſe, to ourſelves in particular: And then we can ſay, "pardon is mine, grace is mine, Chriſt and all his ſpiritual bleſſings are mine." And then we can ſee "our title perfectly clear." (1)

Paul. O my dear Theron! and thus at laſt, you give up your warrant from the written word; (2) as in fact there is no ſuch thing contained in the Bible; and now your recourſe is to the ſpirit. But, if in fact the written word gives you no warrant for this belief—if in fact you have no right by the Bible to lay this claim, the ſpirit of God has nothing to do in the caſe. He cannot clear up a right, where there is no right to be cleared up. He cannot clear up a warrant, where there is no warrant to be cleared up. I grant it is the office of the holy ſpirit to open our underſtandings to underſtand the Scriptures, and to open our eyes to behold the wonderful things in God's Law. But it is not the office of the holy ſpirit, to open our eyes to ſee truths in the Bible, which in fact, are not there. It is not the office of the holy ſpirit to make us believe a lie; that is, believe that the Bible teaches, what in fact, it does not teach; or to make us new revelations, no where contained in Scripture, on which to venture our ſouls for eternity. Nor is it the buſineſs of Faith, to believe theſe new unſcriptural revelations, but only to be-

(1) D. *p.* 295, 362.
(2) *You give up your warrant from the written Word.*—By *the firſt direct act of Faith, antecedent to any reflection, I believe that* "*God is reconciled to me.*" (D. *p.* 169, 362) *If this ſuppoſed truth was contained in and taught by the written word, it was true before I believed it, as all grant: and ſo God was "reconciled to me" before the firſt act of Faith. But they ſay, it was not contained there, it was not true, God was not "reconciled to me" before I believed. But God's Word does not warrant me to believe, as truth, any propoſition, the truth of which is not taught in his Word. All the truths contained in his Word, I ought to believe. But I have no right to add or diminiſh.* Deut. xii. 32. Thou ſhalt not add thereto, nor diminiſh from it. Rev. xxii. 18. *If any man ſhall add unto theſe things, God ſhall add unto him the plagues that are written in this book. If we add to God's Word, we have no warrant from God's Word to believe our additions to be divine. If any doubt of this, let them read.* 2 Theſſ. ii. 11.

lieve with all our hearts, the truths already revealed. Or, to use your own words, "I know no other justifying Faith, but that which relates to the Gospel, and believes its report." But here, sir, lies the wound of your Faith, and this is "the core and root of the controversy," that the thing which you believe, is not revealed in the Bible, nor is there any evidence from Scripture, of the truth of it.— And this you know—this you own, and yet still will persist in believing it, "without any evidence from Scripture, sense, or reason." And to help yourself out, you call in the aid of the holy Spirit, to testify to a thing unrevealed, to a lie, a known lie ; to testify that something is contained in Scripture, which you know is not contained there. That with full assurance, you may say, "pardon is mine, grace is mine, Christ and all his spiritual blessings are mine—consigned over to me in the everlasting Gospel—a title perfectly clear—without any evidence from Scripture, sense, or reason." (1)

Oh my dear Theron ! In matters of this importance, it does not become us to sooth and flatter ; but to speak the truth in uprightness. Did you profess to be an Antinomian, and openly declare, "that the Elect were justified from eternity, or at least from the death of Christ ; that the holy spirit reveals to the Elect their justification in God's own time ; and that justifying Faith consists in believing this new revelation ;" then your scheme, however inconsistent with Scripture, would seem, at least, to be consistent with itself. But now, as you state things, you are (forgive me my Theron) you are, I say, neither consistent with Scripture nor with yourself. And your dressing up experimental religion in this light (while Arminians, Pelagians, Socinians, and Infidels, laugh at the delusion) tends only to embolden self-confident hypocrites ; and to leave the poor awakened Sinner, that has any common honesty in his heart, in a more bewildered case than ever. Or if, by your charming and affectionate manner of address, the poor blind Sinner is induced to believe you, he is in infinite danger of being led to settle on a false foundation, to his eternal ruin. For having once believed—Oh dreadful thought !—Having once believed, he must never doubt again. He must watch and

(1) D. *p.* 269, 362. M. *p.* 173.

DIALOGUE II.

pray, fight and ſtrive againſt doubts, with all his might, as the dreadful Agag, that muſt be purſued with fire and ſword. (1) That being once deluded, it is a thouſand to one, but he lives and dies in his deluſion!

Ther. But does not the holy Scripture expreſsly ſpeak of the *Witneſs* and *Seal of the Spirit?* Rom. viii. 16. Eph. 1. 13.

Paul. Yes, it does.—But never—never—as what any had before Faith and juſtification: as is the caſe with you. *Ye were ſealed,* ſays the Apoſtle to the Epheſian Saints. But when? Before they believed? No. AFTER *that ye believed ye were ſealed.* Eph. 1. 13. And had they this ſpirit of adoption, before they were already children?—No. But, *becauſe ye are ſons,* becauſe ye are already members of God's family, therefore, *God hath ſent forth the ſpirit of his Son into your hearts, crying, Abba, Father.* Gal. iv. 6.

So that I muſt needs tell you, my dear Theron, there is not one tittle in the Bible to countenance your ſcheme: But it is all over inconſiſtence, falſehood and deluſion.—And if your heart is no better than your head, you are in an infinitely dreadful ſtate. What your heart is, I do not pretend to ſay. This does not belong to my province. But the ſcheme of religion you plead for, leads directly to deſtruction. And would that pilot be eſteemed an honeſt man, who, for fear of giving offence, ſhould ſit ſilent and ſuffer the ſhip to run upon the rocks—rocks under water, which he knew would daſh the ſhip to pieces in a moment, if not avoided.

Ther. But, is it not impoſſible to truſt in Chriſt, unleſs firſt we believe that Chriſt and all his ſpiritual bleſſings are ours? (2)

Paul. What would you think, my dear Theron, of a Neonomian, or Arminian, to whom you were opening the way of ſalvation by free grace through Jeſus Chriſt, if he ſhould thus reply? "It is impoſſible to truſt in Chriſt and free grace, unleſs firſt for our encouragement, we are conſcious our lives are reformed, our ſins repented of, and that we are diſpoſed ſincerely to endeavour to do our duty. Were I thus prepared, I ſhould dare to truſt in Chriſt, and could hope that God would accept me through him. But without theſe good qualifications, it is impoſſible I ſhould dare to truſt in Chriſt."

(1) D. *p.* 342, 343.   (2) D. *p.* 312.

Ther. I should suppose that his own righteousness was really at the bottom of his Faith, and the very thing that encouraged him to believe. And such a man does not so properly trust in Christ, as in his own righteousness. And a Faith built on a false foundation, is certainly a false Faith.

Paul. And pray, my Theron, what is it that encourages you to trust in Christ? Not any truths revealed in the Gospel; but something of which you have no evidence, from Scripture, sense, or reason. A firm persuasion of this emboldens you to trust in Christ: yea, is so entirely the foundation of your trust, that if appears to you impossible, without this previous persuasion, ever to trust in him. Wherefore, this persuasion is at the bottom of your trust. And, strictly speaking, you do not so properly trust in Christ, as in that persuasion. Should you now be convinced, that this persuasion was a mere delusion, your trusting in Christ would cease in a moment. Just as it is with a self-righteous person, when his eyes are open to see himself. Rom. vii. 9. *The Commandment came, sin revived, and I died.*

Ther. But, "would any person of the least prudence, erect his house upon a piece of ground, without a previous conviction, that the spot was his own." (1)

Paul. Wherefore then, we must thus conclude, that all the truths, already plainly revealed in the Gospel, which are true before we believe them, and whether we believe them or not; that all these truths laid together, although clearly understood, seen in their spiritual glory, firmly believed, approved of and liked, would not be sufficient to encourage a sinner to trust in Christ. i. e. There is nothing in the written word, which, let it be ever so well understood, and ever so firmly believed, is sufficient to encourage even a regenerate sinner (for it is plain, regeneration is before the first act of Faith. Joh. 1, 12, 13) to trust in Christ. To supply this defect, we must first believe as truth, what as yet is not true, and that without any evidence from Scripture, sense, or reason. And this belief, this persuasion, is to be the foundation of our trusting in Christ; so entirely the foundation, that without it, we cannot "with the least prudence" trust in him. And the weight, the whole weight of our eternal salvation is at

(1) D. *Edit. 1st vol. iii. p.* 285.

DIALOGUE II.

bottom laid, not on the Gospel, the written Gospel, but on a supposed truth, we have no evidence of, from Scripture, sense, or reason.

Oh, my dear Theron! This is a precarious foundation to venture your precious, your immortal soul upon. And should it give way and break under you, it might let you fall down into eternal ruin. This, this is indeed, to use your Aspasio's beautiful similitude, "like placing the dome of a cathedral on the stalk of a tulip."

Mean while let me tell you, the inspired Apostles verily believed, that in the written word we have, not only full evidence of the truth of the Gospel itself (Joh. xx. 31.) but also, the truth of the Gospel being seen, sufficient encouragement to come to God through Christ, in full assurance of being accepted through him. (Heb. x. 19, 22.) And on this ground they preached the Gospel to the world, inviting all to return to God through Jesus Christ; without ever giving the least intimation of any need of their being previously persuaded of some things as truths, which were no where plainly contained in the Gospel.

Ther. Pray, what is there contained in the Gospel which may be sufficient to encourage a Sinner, to return to God through Christ, with full assurance of acceptance thro' him?

Paul. These three truths are set in the clearest and strongest light, in the glorious Gospel of Jesus Christ.

1. That the goodness of God, the supreme governor of the world, is self-moving, and infinite. It needs no external motive, no goodness in us, to draw it forth into exercise. Yea, it can surmount infinite ill-desert—Self-moved. This is demonstrated in God's giving his Son, of his own mere motion, to die for a world, so ill-deserving —infinitely ill-deserving: that no atonement appeared to him sufficient to secure the honour of his law and government, but the blood of his own Son. Let me believe with all my heart, that God has done this deed, a deed infinitely superior to the creation of millions of such worlds as this, all which, with one word's speaking, Messiah could have created in a moment. I say, let me believe with all my heart, that God, of his own mere motion, has given his Son, one equal to himself, to die for such a world as this; and at once I have the fullest conviction of his self-moving goodness, and infinite grace. It stands in a light brighter than the sun at noon-day.

2. God can confiftently with the honour of himfelf, of his law and government, and facred authority, pardon and fave thofe, who, ftrictly fpeaking, are infinitely ill-deferving, through Jefus Chrift, his Son. His honour is, in every point of light, effectually fecured by the mediation and death of his Son. The dignity, the infinite dignity of the fon of God, proves this to the enlightened foul.— The refurrection of Chrift from the dead, is a vifible demonftration of it. And God himfelf, in plain words, declares it to be true:—That he can now be *juft, and yet juftify him that believeth in Jefus.* (Rom. iii. 24, 25, 26.) Now, if the goodnefs of the divine nature is infinite and felf-moving; and if he can, confiftently with his own honour, pardon and fave the infinitely ill-deferving through Jefus Chrift his Son; the only queftion that remains, is, Who may, among all the fons of Adam, truft in this glorious Mediator, return home to God through him, and through his merits and atonement look to the free grace of God for pardon and eternal life?—But,

3. It is moft exprefsly declared, that *whofoever will, may come* (Rev. xxii. 17.) and *he that cometh fhall in no wife be caft out.* (Joh. vi. 37.) Yea, orders are given that thefe glad tidings fhould be carried all round the world, *the Gofpel preached to every creature.* (Mar. xvi. 15.) And all, even the vileft and the worft, are to be, as it were, compelled to come in (Luk. xiv. 23.) *prayed and befeeched to be reconciled to God* (2 Cor. v. 20.) *to repent and be converted* (Act. iii. 19.) to return home to God through Jefus Chrift, to God, who is as ready to be reconciled to the returning Sinner, as the father of the prodigal is reprefented to be, to his returning Son. (Luk. xv. 20.)

Now, when the Sinners eyes, in regeneration, are opened, to behold as in a glafs the glory of the Lord, it will immediately appear to him the fitteft and happieft thing in the world, to return home to God, and be forever devoted to him, if he may. And a clear fight and firm belief of thefe plain Gofpel-truths, gives him the fulleft affurance that he may; that it is God's will he fhould; and that God ftands ready to accept him through Jefus Chrift, if he does. (1)

(1) *Except my eyes are firft opened to behold the glory of God, I cannot fee the ground and reafon of the Law, nor heartily*

Indeed, I readily grant, that unregenerate Sinners do neither see the infinite amiableness of God, nor really believe the Gospel to be true. *The vail is on their hearts.* (2 Cor. iii. 16.) The Gospel *is hid from them.* (Matth. xi. 25.) They are *blind.* (Rom. xi. 25.) And their blindness is a vicious wicked blindness, arising from a heart void of love to God, and full of enmity against his Law, and against the glorious Gospel of his Son; as was proved in our former conversation. And in this benighted state,

approve it as holy, just and good. Unless the law appears good and glorious, I cannot see the wisdom of God in the death of his Son, nor cordially believe the Gospel to be true. Till I see the Gospel to be true, I am blind to the only door of Hope. Merely a sight of the glory of God as a righteous lawgiver, and a sight of the glory of his holy Law, can give no hope. The truth of the Gospel is seen, I then behold (first.) *The love, the self-moving goodness of God, in the gift of his Son: But not, that he loves me in particular, and is reconciled to me.* Secondly, *I then see, that Christ has secured the honour of the divine government; and that now God can be just, and yet justify the Sinner that believeth in Jesus: But not, that I am one for whom he died, with an absolute design to save.* Thirdly, *I then see, that any Sinner may return to God through Christ; and see that those who do, will be accepted and saved: but not, that "pardon is mine, grace is mine, Christ and all his spiritual blessings are mine." In a word, I see the truth of what is already revealed in the Gospel: but I do not see truths not revealed there. The holy Spirit helps me to see the truths already revealed; but reveals no new truths. The things which I believe, were true before I believed them. If, after all, any pretend, there is no difference between these two kinds of Faith; I only say, if these two kinds of Faith, like two roads which seem, and but seem, to lead the same way, should, in fact, lead to two different worlds, as far asunder as Heaven and Hell; it is proper to set up these monuments, to warn travellers: and the nearer they are alike, the more need poor travellers have to take heed they do not mistake. But if they do, if they will mistake after warning, their blood will be upon their own heads: and they will eternally remember, that they knew, what they believed, was not revealed in Scripture. They believed without any evidence from Scripture, sense or reason.*

H

being followed with the fears of eternal misery, they must take some way for hope and comfort. Some go about to establish their own righteousness; and on that, build their hopes for Heaven. Others finding no comfort in the way of duties, try to work up themselves to a belief, that Christ died for them in particular, that God loves them and will save them. And if by any means, they come to feel a strong persuasion of this, it so delivers them from their fears, and so fills them with comfort and joy, that they do all they can to strengthen this persuasion: And to this end, apply an hundred texts of Scripture, perverting them from their plain and natural meaning. And are yet obliged at last to own, that they have no evidence, on which to ground their belief, from Scripture, sense, or reason: Yea, that the thing they believe, is not true, till it becomes true by their believing it to be true. However, their consciences being quieted by this belief, they can now go on, estranged from a God of infinite glory, blind to his infinite beauties: Nor do they believe, that ever any did love God for his own infinite loveliness; although this is the very spirit of all the Angels and Saints in Heaven, and of all good men upon Earth. Isai. vi. 3. 2 Cor. iii. 18. (1)

(1) *To make the matter, if possible, still plainer, it may be thus stated;* 1st. *He that is encouraged to come to Christ from a consciousness of some good qualification in himself, secretly builds his hopes of acceptance with God on his own righteousness.* 2d. *He that is encouraged to come to Christ from a belief that Christ died for him in particular, and that God is reconciled to him, builds his hopes of acceptance with God on a delusion.* 3d. *He that comes to Christ without a disposition to be reconciled to God, is only seeking after salvation from Hell, and does not desire the salvation which the Gospel offers.* 4th. *He that thinks he has a disposition to be reconciled to God, but never saw the glory of God, of his law and government, he but deceives himself.* 5th. *He that is encouraged to come, only by the free grace of God through Jesus Christ, as revealed in the written word, builds his hopes of acceptance on the truth. He that comes on this encouragement, with a hearty disposition to be forever reconciled to God, and devoted to him, and thirsting for grace forever to live to him, is a true convert. He that, after this, lives to God through all trials, proves his faith by his works, as Abraham did.*—Gen. xxii. 12.

DIALOGUE II.

Ther. I see you are returned again to your darling topic, the doctrine of loving God for his own loveliness.

Paul. Yes—And this is the very vitals of vital piety. A sense of the beauty of the divine nature, and a firm belief of the truth of the Gospel, lay the foundation for all the rest. (Joh. xvii. 3.) *Repentance towards God, Faith towards our Lord Jesus Christ,* a life of communion with God and devotedness to him, joy in God, and rejoicing in Jesus Christ. And while the love of God—not a belief that God loves me in particular, without any evidence from Scripture, sense, or reason, but a clear and lively sense of the self-moving goodness and infinite grace of God, as manifested in the gift of his Son, and shining forth in the whole Gospel-way of life, as exhibited in the written word, is shed abroad in our hearts by the Holy Ghost; attended with a full assurance that we are the children of God, resulting from a consciousness of a filial spirit towards God; now we know and believe the love that God hath to us. And inspired with a sense of the divine glory, the beauty of God's Law and government, the glory of the way of salvation by free grace through Jesus Christ, the free and sovereign grace of God in calling us into the kingdom of his Son, we rejoice with joy unspeakable and full of glory: And habitually, and actually, through the course of our lives, present ourselves a living sacrifice to God through Jesus Christ; to be for him, entirely for him, and that forever. Nor do we feel any need to bring your kind of Faith into the account.

You remember, my dear Theron, that parabolical picture of a true Saint, of a real Christian, given by our blessed Saviour, in Matth. xiii. 23. whose representations, if we do not believe, we do indeed make God a liar. *He that received seed into the good ground, is he*—not that hath a new revelation of a new truth not contained in the Gospel! But is he *that heareth the word, and*—what next? Not, is really persuaded in his heart, that " pardon is mine, grace is mine, Christ and all his spiritual blessings are mine,"! without any evidence " from Scripture, sense, or reason" But, heareth the word and *understandeth it so as in it, to behold as in a glass, the glory of the Lord. Which also*—what? Complains that his graces are no more to be seen " than the stars at noon"! No, what then? *Which alſo beareth fruit.*—How much? So little that no eye can ſee it! Or at moſt, but juſt diſcern it, "as a glow-worm in the night"! And that in ſo unſteady, uncertain a manner, that for his life he cannot tell whether there be any fruit or no; but rather the more he looks, the more "his doubts are increaſed? (1) No, no, far from this—*and bringeth forth ſome a hundred fold, ſome ſixty, ſome thirty.*—Yes, my Theron, that is good ground indeed, which yields an hundred buſhels of grain, for one that was ſown; or ſixty, or even thirty.—And thus, *the grain of muſtard ſeed, becometh a great tree.* (Ver. 31, 32.) And thus, *the leaven ſpreads till the whole is leavened.* (Ver. 33.) And this is the idea, the grand and noble idea, our bleſſed Saviour had of a true Chriſtian!—It is granted, there is great difference in the degrees of fruitfulneſs in true converts, ſome an hundred fold, ſome ſixty, ſome thirty.—But thoſe who bring forth no good fruit, whatever raviſhing joys they may ſometimes have had (Ver. 20) are by our bleſſed Saviour pictured by the ſimilitude of—*ſtony ground—thorny ground.*

Ther. But I have an unanſwerable objection againſt this account of the nature of juſtifying Faith. For, whereas in the holy Scriptures it is repreſented to be an exceeding difficult thing to believe; according to you, there is no difficulty at all in it, when once the Sinner, in your ſenſe of things, is regenerate, and believes the Goſpel to be true with all his heart.

Paul. Right, my dear Theron. The difficulty is now over. For he is not obliged to believe "without any evidence from Scripture, ſenſe, or reaſon." The way in which he is to return to God, all lies open, plain before him. And it appears to him the fitteſt and happieſt thing in the world, to return home to God through Jeſus Chriſt. And he does it with all his heart. (2)

(1) D. *p.* 361, 362.
(2) *Return home to God—By this phraſe Paulinus means exactly the ſame with thoſe words in Jer. iv.* 1. *If thou wilt return, O Iſrael, ſaith the Lord, return unto me. And in Ezek. xxxiii.* 11. *Turn ye, turn ye from your evil ways; for why will ye die! And in Act. iii.* 19.--*Repent and be converted, that your ſins may be blotted out. From being enemies, repent and turn, and be reconciled to God,* 2 Cor. *v.*

Ther. Wherein then confists the difficulty of believing?

Paul. The difficulty in the way of embracing the Gospel in a saving manner, according to the New Testament, arises from a worldly spirit, a self-righteous spirit, and being dead in sin.

(1) From a worldly spirit: Men are generally so attached to worldly things, riches, honour, and pleasure, that, although they might be glad to know they should go to Heaven when they die, yet they have no heart to become the disciples of Christ; to deny themselves, take up their cross and follow him; and take God for the alone portion of their souls. Therefore, when they are invited to come to this feast (and a feast indeed it is, to a regenerate Sinner, whose eyes are opened to see things as they are) they desire to be *excused*. (Luk. xiv. 18) And they *make light of it, and go their ways, one to his farm, another to his merchandize.* Matth. xxii 5.

(2) From a *self-righteous spirit*. Rom. ix. 31, 32, 33. For if a Sinner is so terrified with the fears of eternal damnation, that he can take no comfort in worldly enjoyments; and so is quite prepared to hear Aspasio urge him to believe, that God loves him, and Christ died for him; yet there now remains the chief difficulty in the way of true Faith, unremoved, viz. to yield the point, that the Law not only does in fact, require sinless perfection, on pain of eternal damnation, and that he is under the curse of this Law, but that this Law is holy, just, and good: And so he justly condemned, and in fact, in the hands, and at the disposal of a sovereign God. This—this—a proud self-righteous spirit, is diametrically opposite unto.

20.——*It is worthy to be observed, that according to St. Peter repentance is before forgiveness.* Repent and be converted, that your sins MAY be blotted out. *And this is the doctrine God as taught in all ages of the world. By Moses, Lev. xxvi.* 40.—*By David, Psal. xxxii.* 5.—*By Isaiah. Isai. lv.* 7.—*By John Baptist, Mar. i.* 4.—*By Christ, Matth. v.* 4. *Luk. xiii.* 3.— *By all the Apostles on the day of Pentecost, Act. ii.* 37, 38, 39. *and indeed all over the Scripture. But there is nothing of the nature of repentance before forgiveness in Theron's scheme. Yea, his repentance, professedly, arises wholly from a belief that his sins are forgiven. So that he is forgiven before he begins to repent.*

H 3

And to be brought to this, is killing work. Rom. vii. 9. *The commandment came, sin revived, and I died.*

(3) From being spiritually dead :—For when the Law has thoroughly done its work, and the Sinner sees and feels the truth, that he is dead in sin, justly condemned, absolutely helpless and undone in himself, in the hands of a sovereign God, who *hath mercy on whom he will have mercy*—there now needs the same mighty power whereby Christ was raised from the dead, to quicken this dead Sinner. And it must wholly proceed from the mere free sovereign grace of God. (Eph. i. 19, 20, compared with Eph. ii. 1, 8.) That regeneration does thus precede the first act of Faith, is plain from Joh. i. 12, 13, where concerning all true believers, it is said, *which were born—*that is, antecedent to the first act of Faith—*which were born, not of blood, nor of the will of the flesh, nor of the will of man, but of God.* See also Joh. iii. 3, 5.

But these three difficulties being removed, and Sinners made *willing in the day of his power* (Psal. cx. 3.) all is easy. Sinners now *come flying* to Christ, as naturally *as doves to their windows.* (Isai. lx. 8.) For God appears to be infinitely glorious, and the Gospel to be divinely true.

And here, by the way, my dear Theron, it is worthy of your diligent attention, that it is a common thing in the New-Testament, to promise salvation to those, who believe the truth of the Gospel with all their hearts, and to speak of such, as true Saints : Because where this is, every thing else will follow of course. In this view, you may at your leisure, read the following Scriptures. Matth. xvi. 16. 17. Mar xvi, 15, 16. Joh. vi. 68, 69, and xvii. 3, 8, and xx. 30, 31. Act. viii. 37. Rom. x. 9. 1 Cor. xii. 3. 1 Joh. iv, 15, and v. 1, 5. Some of which are sadly perverted by some writers; particularly, Rom. x. 9. (1)

Ther. The clock strikes nine—It is time for me to retire —However, before I go, pray point out, in brief, the chief differences between what you call true Faith, and the Faith I have been pleading for that I may have them to consider at my leisure. For I design more thoroughly to look into this matter, than ever yet I have done.

Paul. Among the many differences which might be mentioned, I will only point out these twelve.

(1) D. *p.* 291. *Marrow of Mod. Div. Notes, p.* 155, 156.

(1) Regeneration is neceſſarily previous to the firſt act of true Faith. But your Faith may exiſt in an unregenerate heart.

(2) True Faith ſuppoſes the Law and Goſpel are rightly underſtood, and beheld in their glory; the Law approved with all the heart, as holy, juſt, and good; the Goſpel believed, and complied with, with all the heart. But your Faith is confiſtent with a reigning enmity againſt both Law and Goſpel.

(3) True Faith is an holy act. But yours has nothing of the nature of holineſs in it; ariſes from no higher principle than ſelf-love.

(4) In true Faith, nothing is believed but what is plainly revealed in the holy Scriptures. But in your Faith, the main things believed, are no where contained in the Bible. "Pardon is mine, grace is mine, Chriſt and all his ſpiritual bleſſings are mine."

(5) In true Faith, the things believed were as true, before they were believed, as after; being all contained in the Scriptures of truth. But in your Faith, the things believed were not true, before they were believed; not being contained in the Bible.

(6) True Faith is founded wholly on that revelation, which is made in the written word. But your Faith, having no ſupport from Scripture, ſenſe, or reaſon, is founded wholly in a heated Imagination; or, which is no better, on a new revelation, not contained in the written word: i. e. One is founded on good evidence, the other not.

(7) The great difficulty in the way of true Faith, ariſes from the wickedneſs of the heart. But the great difficulty in the way of your Faith, is, that there is no evidence of the truth of the thing believed, from Scripture, ſenſe, or reaſon: But rather, a man is obliged to go contrary to them all.

(8) True Faith is wrought in the heart by the holy ſpirit, in regeneration, imparting divine life to the dead ſoul, opening the eyes to behold divine truths in their glory and reality: In conſequence of which, the Goſpel is underſtood, believed, and embraced with all the heart. But your Faith is wrought by your being made, by ſome means or other, to believe ſome things as true, that are not revealed in Scripture.

(9) In true Faith, the way of ſalvation by free grace through Jeſus Chriſt, being underſtood and believed, is

heartily approved of, and acquiesced in, as being glorious for God and safe for the Sinner : And our entire dependence for acceptance with God, is on the free grace of God through Jesus Christ, as exhibited in the written word. Whereas, your Faith does not properly consist in dependence, but in confidence.—Not in looking to the free grace of God through Jesus Christ, that you may be pardoned, sanctified and saved ; not in flying for refuge, and laying hold on this hope set before you ; but in being confident, that "pardon is mine, grace is mine, Christ and all his spiritual blessings are mine." In being " really persuaded in my heart, that Christ is mine, and that I shall have life and salvation by him"; without any evidence " from Scripture, sense, or reason." (1)

(10) True Faith is always attended with love to God, arising from a sense of his own infinite amiableness, as its inseparable concomitant. Your Faith is sometimes followed with a seeming love to God, arising merely from believing that he loves you.

(11) But the most remarkable difference of all, is, that true Faith actually unites the man to Jesus Christ, as the *branch is united to the vine*. (Joh. xv. 5.) In consequence of which, every true believer actually receives the spirit of Christ to *dwell in him*. (2) Rom. viii. 9. Eph. i. 13. Gal. iii. 2, 14. 1 Joh. iv, 13, and ii. 27. Rom. viii. 14.

(1) *I grant, that writers on that side of the question, speak much of trusting in Christ, and resting upon him, &c. Yet according to them, previous to this trust, and that which encourages to it, is a belief that "pardon is mine, grace is mine, Christ and all his spiritual blessings are mine." And so I believe that my sins are pardoned, before I begin to trust in Christ. I do not come to Christ, but rather stand off and keep at a distance, till I see he is mine, and can call God, my God. So that strictly speaking, I am justified, and know that I am justified, before I dare come to Christ, and trust in him. Thus the matter is stated, in—*D. p. 312.

(2) *Although it is plain from Scripture, that regeneration is before the first act of saving Faith (Joh. i. 12, 13.) And that Faith is wrought by the influences of the holy spirit (Eph. i. 19.) Yet it is equally plain, that the gift of the holy spirit, to dwell in us, as an abiding principle of divine life, is after we are united to Christ by Faith (Eph. i. 13. Gal. iii. 14.)*

Gal. v. 18. In consequence of this, a certain foundation is laid, to bring *forth fruit* unto God (Rom. vii. 4.) in every instance (Matth. xiii. 23.) And *the path of the just is as the shining light, which shineth more and more unto the perfect day.* (Prov. iv. 18.) *If he faileth, he riseth up again.* (Prov. xxiv. 16.) *Every branch that beareth fruit,* GOD *purgeth* it, and so *it bringeth forth more fruit.* (Joh. xv. 2.) Whence, near or quite all the Saints we read of in Scripture, usually speak the language of assurance, as being conscious to this divine habitual change wrought in them by God's holy spirit. But thus it is not with your kind of Faith. Nor is assurance this way to be obtained on your scheme.

(12) As a natural consequence of the whole, the several systems of experimental religion, resulting from these two kinds of Faith, however in appearance they may be alike, yet in reality, are essentially different throughout. While the true believer is striving to grow in grace, the false pretender is striving to maintain his delusion.——

Ther. I thank you, sir, for present instructions; and with your leave I will return to-morrow evening; as I want to hear your thoughts on one subject more.

Paul. The evening shall be at your service, God willing.

So ended the second conversation, and I retired again to my closet—with what views of my spiritual state, you may easily guess.—Oh, my dear Aspasio!—What! Are we all wrong! Or have I misunderstood your scheme! I hope, I wish, no poor Sinner on earth was ever so deluded as I have been.—The Lord have mercy on me!—O, my dear Aspasio, that you had been present, and heard all that passed!—But alas, the wide ocean keeps us three thousand miles apart! However, with you, even now with you, is the distressed heart of

Your disconsolate

THERON.

After union to Christ we have a covenant-right to the holy spirit (Gal. iii. 29.) may have divine grace, at any time, for asking (Luk. xi. 13.) But before union with Christ, we have no right—God is at absolute liberty—we lie at his sovereign mercy, (Rom. ix. 15. 18.) And accordingly, regenerating grace is the effect of his sovereign good pleasure, (Matth. xi. 25, 26.) No promises of saving grace are made to the prayers or doings of Sinners out of Christ, (Gal. iii. 10. 2 Cor. i. 20. Joh. iii. 18, 36.

DIALOGUE III.

Wednesday Evening, December 13, 1758.

ACCORDING to appointment, I made my third visit. The subject proposed was the doctrine of ASSURANCE. We soon entered upon it; and this is the sum of what passed:

Ther. May the people of God, in this life, attain to a certain assurance, that they are in a state of favour with God, and entitled to eternal glory?

Paul. As there is a specific difference between true grace and all counterfeits; as true grace in the heart is naturally discernible, like all our other inward biasses; as the Saints in Scripture usually speak the language of assurance; as Saints in all ages are exhorted to seek assurance (2 Pet. i. 10.) and as there are many rules laid down in Scripture to determine in this case, and many promises made for the encouragement of Saints, the designed advantage of which cannot be enjoyed without assurance; so, for these and other reasons, I believe, that assurance is attainable, in this life, in all ordinary cases at least.

Ther. How, and by what means may the children of God attain assurance?

Paul. Sanctification, taking the word in a large and comprehensive sense, is the evidence, the only Scripture-evidence of a good estate.

Ther. What do you mean by sanctification, in this large and comprehensive sense?

Paul. It is usual for divines to distinguish between regeneration and conversion; between first conversion and progressive sanctification; between divine views and holy affections; between grace in the heart, and an holy life and conversation; but I mean to comprehend all under one general name. You may call it the image of God, or holiness of heart and life, or a real conformity to the divine Law, and a genuine compliance with the Gospel of Christ. I have already let you see what I apprehend to be the nature of Law and Gospel, of love to God and Faith in Christ. When I say, this is the only evidence, I mean, that this is the only thing, wherein Saints and Sinners, in every instance differ. One has the image of God, the other has not. Or, to express myself in the language of inspiration (Joh. xvii. 3.) *This is life eternal, to know thee, the only true God, and Jesus Christ whom thou hast sent.* And (1 Joh. ii. 3, 4, 5.) *Hereby we do know that we know him, if we keep his commandments. He that saith, I know him, and keepeth not his commandments, is a liar, and the truth is not in him. But whoso keepeth his word, in him verily is the love of God perfected: Hereby know we that we are in him.*

Ther. What is the best method a true Saint can take, to maintain a constant assurance of his good estate?

Paul. To live in the exercise of all Christian graces in his own heart every day, and to be constantly influenced and governed by them in all his external conduct in the world: *Growing in grace, and pressing forward to perfection.* 2 Pet. i. 5, 11.

Ther. But is it possible, that all true Saints should live so?

Paul. Why not?—For, they are all delivered from the power of sin, (Rom. vi. 2, 14.) are married to Christ, in whom all fullness dwells, (Rom. vii. 4.) have already every principle of grace in their hearts, (Joh. i. 15.) and the spirit of God actually dwelling in them (Rom. viii. 9.) and constantly influencing them, to such a degree, that they do not, they even cannot, feel and live as others do (1 Joh. iii. 9. (1)

(1) 1 Joh. iii. 9. *Whosoever is born of God, doth not commit sin: for his seed remaineth in him: and he cannot sin, because he is born of God.—He doth not, and he cannot, at any time: for his seed always remaineth in him. So that these words teach us, that there is at all times a real difference between a Saint and a Sinner.*

It is true, there is no particular bias or inclination, whether natural or gracious, in the heart of man, but may be counteracted. But to counteract the habitual bias of the heart, is quite different from acting agreeably to the habitual yea actually carrying on the work of sanctification. (Joh. xv. 2.)—The God of all grace ready, mean while, to grant all further needful help, as ready as ever a kind parent was to give bread to a hungry child. (Matth. vii. 7, 11.) So that they are completely furnished to live daily in the exercise of every grace. (Eph. ii. 10.) Yea, this is expected of them, as they would act up to their proper character. (Eph. iv. 1.) Yea, I will venture to add, having so good an authority as the Son of God, that, though there are different degrees of grace and fruitfulness among true Saints, yet it is their common character to *bring forth fruit, some an hundred fold, some sixty, some thirty.* (Matth. viii. 23.) So that it seems more difficult to reconcile it with Scripture, that a true Saint (there being no extraordinary bodily disease, as the hypochondria, &c. nor other extraordinary circumstances, that may account for it) should live along in the dark, full of doubts and fears about his state, from year to year; I say, more difficult to reconcile this with Scripture, than it is to prove that they may live so, as to make their calling and election sure, according to that exhortation in 2 Pet. i. 5, 11.

bias *of the heart. The Saint counteracts the habitual bias of his heart, when he sins. The Sinner acts agreeable to the habitual bias of his whole heart, when he sins. So a Saint never sins with all his heart, as the wicked man does. He cannot, because his seed remains in him; because he is born of God. The spirit lusteth against the flesh; so that he cannot. Gal. v. 17.*

Therefore good men, when they fall, are restless till they come to repentance; as was the case with David. Psal. xxxii. 3, 4, 5. For they are out of their element; all is vanity and vexation of spirit; as was the case with Solomon. Eccl. 1, 2. As when Haman led Mordecai through the street of Shushan, on the king's horse, dressed in the royal apparel, and proclaimed his honours in the ears of the people, he acted exceeding contrary to the habitual bias of his heart. Esth. vi.— So did Peter, when he denied his master; and therefore at one look of Christ, he went out and wept bitterly. So that these instances, though often alledged, are not to the purpose of stoney-ground hearers. For they have no root in themselves.— They receive the word with joy, endure for a while, and fall away. Matth. xiii. 20, 21.—See Mr. Edwards on Religious Affections, p. 274, 277.

Ther. But I have known some, esteemed true converts, who after their conversion, have lain dead, without any sensible divine influence, for months together.

Paul. Why did not you add,—and years together?— For once I knew of one, counted an eminent Christian, who declared he lay dead twelve years, without one act of grace all that time. But what good do such conversions do? If men are as much under the power of spiritual death after their conversions, as before, what benefit is there in being converted? And what becomes of all those Scriptures, which declare, *He shall save his people from their sins.* Matth. i. 21. *That we might serve him, without fear, in holiness and righteousness all the days of our lives.* Luk. i. 43. *A new heart will I give you, and a new spirit will I put within you, and I will take away the stony heart out of your flesh, and I will give you an heart of flesh: and I will put my spirit within you, and cause you to walk in my statutes, and ye shall keep my judgments, and do them.* Ezek. xxxvi. 26, 27. *Who gave himself for us, that he might redeem us from all iniquity, and purify unto himself a peculiar people, zealous of good works.* Tit. ii. 14.—And pray take notice, my dear Theron, that, as God gave the law written on tables of stone, to Israel, to all *Israel according to the flesh,* which covenant (Deut. ix. 9, 15,) they did break (Heb. viii. 9,) so he has expressly promised to all the *spiritual Israel,* i. e. to all true believers (Gal. iii. 29,) that he will *write his law in their hearts;* i. e. give them an inward temper of mind answerable to his written law. Heb. viii. 10. A hypocrite may go to God and say, " pardon is mine, grace is mine," and be ravished with his own delusion : but God doth, in fact, write his law in the heart of every true believer. This is God's mark, put upon all that are of his flock; whereby his sheep are distinguished from the rest of the world.

Ther. But cannot a man, who is very uncertain of his sanctification, be sure of eternal life some other way?

Paul. Our Saviour having described the Christian temper and life, in his Sermon on the Mount, concludes with the strongest assurances, that such, and such only, as are truely sanctified, shall be finally saved. If we are such, our *house is built upon a rock;* if not, our *house is built upon the sand.*—Now, my dear Theron, we hope to go to Heaven when we die. So do many, who will be finally

I

disappointed. How shall you and I know, that our foundation is good? Who can tell us? Surely none better than he who is to be our judge. Could we ask our blessed Saviour, LORD, how shall we know? What would he say? Thanks be to God, we know what he would say, as surely as though he should answer us with an audible voice from Heaven. For he is now of the same mind, as when he dwelt on earth. What he then taught, is left on record, plain for all to read, that none might mistake in a point of such infinite importance.

Take your Bible, my dear Theron, read our Saviour's Sermon on the Mount; and there you will see the character of a true Christian, drawn by an infallible hand; and find a test, by which you may safely try your state. The true Christian is *humble, penitent, meek, longing after holiness, merciful, pure in heart, a peace-maker, willing to part with all for Christ, and to go through the greatest sufferings in his cause*. Matth. v. 1, 12. Like *salt*, he is full of life and spirit: Like *light*, by his knowledge and example, he enlightens all around him, and is an *honour* to his master (Ver. 13, 16,) lives by a *stricter rule* than any *hypocrite*— (Ver. 20,) does not justify nor indulge the *least grudge* against his neighbour, or the *first stirrings of any corruption* in his heart (Ver. 21, 42,) *loves* not only his friends, but *his enemies*, even *his worst enemies* (Ver. 43, 48,) *gives alms* and *prays*, as in the *sight of God* (Chap. vi. 1, 5,) is *chiefly concerned* for the *honour* of God, and *kingdom* and *interest* of Christ in the world (Ver. 9, 10,) chuses God for his *portion*, lays up his treasure in Heaven, and means with an honest heart, with a *single eye*, only to be God's servant; and *trusting* his kind providence for temporal supplies he makes it his chief business to be truly religious. Ver. 19, 34. Not of a carping, captious, censorious disposition; but chiefly attentive to, and mostly concerned to amend his own faults. Chap. vii. 1, 5. He prays and his prayers are answered. Ver. 7, 11. And in imitation of the divine goodness, he is kind to all around him, *doing as he would be done by*. Ver. 12. At his conversion, he enters in at this *strait Gate* of strict piety, and through the course of his life, he travels in this *narrow way* of holiness, almost alone, few suited with that road, many walking in *broader ways*. Ver. 13, 14. Nor will he be diverted from these sentiments and ways, by any preachers or writers, whatever appearances of holiness and devotion they may put on. Ver. 15.

Ther. But do you really and verily believe, that none will at last be admitted into Heaven, but those who are of this character?

Paul. Pray, my dear Theron, read our Saviour's answer to your question, and believe it.—Believe that he means as he says.

Ther. Not every one that saith unto me, Lord, Lord, shall enter into the kingdom of Heaven: but he that doth the will of my Father which is in Heaven. Ver. 21.

Paul. Observe, that DOTH, not that DID some years ago.—But that DOTH, through the course of his life.—Forgive this interruption.—Pray read on——

Ther. Many will say to me in that day, Lord, Lord, have we not prophesied in thy name? And in thy name cast out Devils? And in thy name done many wonderful works?— Ver. 22.

Paul. You see they are in confident expectation of eternal life. But what is their doom?

Ther. And then will I profess unto them, I never knew you: depart from me, ye that work iniquity. Therefore, whosoever heareth these sayings of mine, and doth them, I will liken him unto a wise man, which built his house upon a rock: and the rain descended, and the floods came, and the winds blew, and beat upon that house: and it fell not, for it was founded upon a rock. And every one that heareth these sayings of mine, and doth them not, shall be likened unto a foolish man, which built his house upon the sand: and the rains descended, and the floods came, and the winds blew, and beat upon that house: and it fell, and great was the fall of it. Ver. 23, 27.

Paul. Observe, my dear Theron, our Saviour does not say, every one who firmly believeth that he shall be saved, however unconscious of sanctifying operations in his own breast, shall, as sure as God is true, be forever happy.—No—but just the reverse. He says, that however confident men be of salvation, yet if they do not the things contained in his sermon, their hopes shall infallibly be disappointed. Now say, my dear Theron, do you believe this doctrine, taught by our blessed Saviour?

Ther. I must own, I have not been wont to view things just in this light. "I used to think, I need not trouble myself, to find out a multitude of marks and signs of true grace, if I could find a few good ones. Particularly, I thought I might know I was passed from death to life, if I loved the brethren." (1)

Paul. Your few good ones are all counterfeit, if alone, separate from other good ones. For the true Saint receives every grace from Christ. Joh. i. 16. Nor did Christ mean to single out a few in his sermon, but to give a brief summary of the whole Christian life. And *he that heareth these sayings of mine, and doth them*—not, doth a few of them—but doth them one and all. Read through the first Epistle of John, and you will see this sentiment confirmed.—Where there is one grace, there is all. If there is not all, there is none. (2)

Ther. But, Sir, suffer me to tell you, that "this method of seeking peace and assurance, I fear, will perplex the simple minded; and cherish rather than suppress, the fluctuations of doubt. For, let the signs be what you please, a love of the brethren, or a love of all righteousness, a change of heart, or an alteration of life; these good qualifications are sometimes like the stars at noon-day, not easily, if at all, discernible; or else they are like a glow-worm in the night, glimmering, rather than shining:—Consequently will yield at the best, but a feeble—at the worst, a very precarious evidence. If, in such a manner, we should acquire some little assurance, how soon may it be unsettled by the incursions of daily temptations, or destroyed by the insurrection of remaining sin! At such a juncture, how will it keep its standing! How retain its being! It will fare like a tottering wall, before a tempest;

(1) M. *p.* 291, 292.
(2) *However on the Arminian and Antinomian schemes of religion, in which nothing is truly harmonious and consistent, what they call graces, may, some particulars of them be found alone; yet on St. Paul's scheme this can never happen. For every grace natively results from those divine views, which lay the foundation of any one grace.* Beholding as in a glass the glory of the Lord, *as shining forth in the law and in the Gospel,* we are changed into the same image,---*i. e. into a real conformity to the law, and a genuine compliance with the Gospel, comprising all the branches of religion.* See Mr. Edwards on *Religious Affections, p.* 249, 261.

or be *as the rush without mire, and the flag without water.* Job viii. 11.

"Inſtead therefore of poring on our own hearts, to diſcover, by inherent qualities, our intereſt in Chriſt, I ſhould rather renew my application to the free and faithful promiſe of the Lord : aſſert and maintain my title on this unalterable ground. Pardon is mine, I would ſay, grace is mine, Chriſt and all his ſpiritual bleſſings are mine.—— Why? Becauſe I am conſcious of ſanctifying operations in my own breaſt. Rather, becauſe God hath ſpoken in his holineſs; becauſe all theſe precious privileges are conſigned over to me in the everlaſting Goſpel, with a clearneſs unqueſtionable as the truth, with a certainty inviolable as the oath of God." (1)

Paul. But did you not uſe to think, that Faith was productive of good works? Yea, did not your Aſpaſio teach you this doctrine?

Ther. I muſt confeſs he did. This was once the language of my Aſpaſio to me, while I was yet an unbeliever. To give me an exalted idea of Faith, thus he taught me. "Faith will make every power of our ſouls ſpring forward to glorify our heavenly Father—glorify him by every inſtance of obedience, fidelity and zeal. (2) It makes all the powers of our ſouls like the chariots of Amminadib, ready, expedite, and active in duty. (3) This is the love of God, that we walk after his commandments. This is the natural fruit—this the certain evidence of love to that glorious, tranſcendent, and adorable Being. It buildeth up the fair fabric of univerſal Godlineſs." (4) It "will diffuſe itſelf through every intellectual faculty, and extend to every ſpecies of duty, till the whole heart is filled with the image, and the whole behaviour regulated by the law of the bleſſed God." (5) It "will induce us to preſent all the members of our bodies, and all the faculties of our ſouls, as a living ſacrifice to the honour of God, to be employed in his ſervice and reſigned to his will." To "be as pilgrims below, and have our converſation above. Such, my dear Theron," ſaid he to me, "will be the effects of Faith. (6) Nothing is more certain than that Faith

(1) D. *p.* 361, 362   (2) D. *p.* 169.   (3) D. *p.* 176.
(4) D. *p.* 177.   (5) D. *p.* 179.   (6) D. *p.* 181.

is a vital, an operative, a victorious principle. (1) When the first converts believed, the change of their behaviour was so remarkable, the holiness of their lives so exemplary, that they won the favour, and commanded the respect of all the people. Act. ii. 47. In short, it is as impossible for the Sun to be in his meridian sphere, and not to dissipate darkness, or diffuse light, as for Faith to exist in the soul and not exalt the temper, and meliorate the conduct." (2) All which, besides proving it by many texts of Scripture, he illustrated at large, in the example of Saint Paul and Abraham (3) and concluded with assuring me, that Faith " will give life to every religious duty." (4) And make us " abound in the work of the Lord." (5) Yea, at another time he taught me, " that Faith, even when weak, is productive of good works."(6) Which are " the proof," and do "undeniably attest its sincerity." (7) They are "the grand characteristic, which distinguishes the sterling from the counterfeit. (8) They will distinguish the true believer from the hypocritical professor, even at the great tribunal.(9) And at another time, I remember, my Aspasio said, " Do we *love our enemies; bless them that curse us ; do good to them that hate us ; pray for them which despitefully use us, and persecute us?* Without this loving and lovely disposition, *we abide,* says the Apostle, *in death;* are destitute of spiritual, and have no title to eternal life." (10)

Paul. " No title to eternal life" ! How dare you then go to God and say, " pardon is mine, grace is mine, Christ and all his spiritual blessings are mine" !

Ther. This is that very Faith, which my Aspasio taught me to exercise. And which he assured me, would be " as a torch in a sheaf,"(11) in kindling every grace into a sudden flame.

Paul. But why then does not every grace flame out ?—Why is not your heart like the chariots of Amminadib ? And your title to Heaven clear " from a consciousness of sanctifying operations in your own breast"? If your Faith is "a vital, an operative, a victorious principle," why

(1) D. *p.* 182. (2) D. *p.* 182, 183. (3) D. *p.* 187, 203. (4) D. *p.* 206. (5) D. *p.* 207. (6) *Vol. I. Edit. I. p.* 251. (7) *Vol. I. Edit. I. p.* 252. (8) *Vol. I. Edit. I. p.* 259. (9) *Vol. I. Edit. I. p.* 278. (10) *Vol. II. Edit. II. p.* 303. (11) D. *p.* 336.

cannot you obtain a full assurance from that "grand characteristic, which distinguishes the sterling from the counterfeit," in this world; and which "will distinguish the true believer from the hypocritical professor, even at the great tribunal;" And without which, you are in fact "destitute of spiritual, and have no title to eternal life"?

Ther. Once I had this evidence, as I thought, clear in my favour. But by experience I found at length, that no steady lasting assurance could be had this way. For my graces were mostly "as the stars at noon," quite invisible: Or at best, "as a glow-worm in the night," but just to be seen. So that the "little assurance" I had, was very unsteady. Yea, looking for marks of grace, I found "rather increased my doubts;" as I could not but discern more evidences against me, than for me. Therefore I gave up this way, as tending to perpetual uncertainty. And as a more direct way to assurance and peace, I learnt to live by Faith; to go to God, and say, "pardon is mine, &c."

Paul. And all, my dear Theron, "without any evidence from Scripture, sense, or reason." Yea, in direct opposition to your own Aspasio, who affirms, that Faith is "a vital, operative, victorious principle." Pray how do you know, that your Faith is sterling, and not counterfeit?— Be quite impartial, and say, is it not to be feared, that your Faith is what Saint James calls a *dead Faith*?

Ther. But the time once was, when I was full of light, love and joy.

Paul. Yes. Like a "torch in a sheaf," all in a flame of love, to think your sins were pardoned. But you see, that this sort of love, like the Israelites joy at the side of the Red-Sea, does not last long. But like the stony-ground, it endures for a while, and then comes to nothing. And your graces are now no more to be seen than "the stars at noon." And you must give up your assurance, or take another course to support it, and another course, indeed, you take—to live by Faith? "Without any evidence," as Mr. Marshall owns, whose book your Aspasio values next to the Bible—without any evidence "from Scripture, sense, or reason." And is this that glorious Faith, your Aspasio once so highly extolled! Is all come to this at last!

Ther. Yes.—And did not Abraham thus live by Faith? who *against Hope believed in Hope*. Rom. iv. 18. And was not this the way of Saints in general under the old Testament? When *they walked in darkness and saw no light*, they *trusted in the Lord, and stayed themselves on their God.* Isai. l. 10. And was not this the way of Saints in the Apostolic age? *They walked by Faith, and not by sight.* 2 Cor. v. 7. David checked himself for doubting. *Why art thou cast down, O my soul?* Psal. xlii. And Asaph looked upon it as his sin. Psal. lxxvii. 10. *I said, this is my infirmity.*—And Christ often upbraided his disciples for their unbelief. And St. Paul charges the Hebrew converts not to *cast away their confidence.* Heb. x. 25.

Paul. Pray, my dear Theron, take your Bible, and read the several texts you refer to; read what goes before, and what follows after; and you may easily see, not one of them is to your purpose. God had promised to give Abraham a son, although his wife was not only barren, but also by reason of age past child-bearing: and notwithstanding the difficulties in the way of its accomplishment, Abraham believed the divine promise.—God had by the mouth of Samuel promised to give David the kingdom of Israel.—But he was banished from his country, and from God's sanctuary: his enemies taunted; yea, and his life was in continual danger. So that he was ready sometimes to say, *I shall perish one day by the hand of Saul.* But then again he checked himself for giving way to such unreasonable discouragement; after the express promise of God to him. *Why art thou cast down, O my soul!* However, through all the psalm he appears conscious to the exercise of grace in his heart, and discovers not the least doubt of the goodness of his state. See Psal. xlii.—So the captives in Babylon had an express promise, that after seventy years they should return to Zion. But such an event, situate as they were, seemed incredible. Every thing looked dark. They had no light. They saw no way for their return. But God had promised it; and therefore, they (who feared the Lord, and obeyed his voice. i. e. who were " conscious of sanctifying operations in their own breasts") for their encouragement, are exhorted to cast their burden upon their God, and put an implicit faith in his wisdom, power and veracity; and trust in him to accomplish his word. (Read from Isai. xlix. 13. to Isai. l. 10.)—So Asaph knew he was a sincere godly man; as is evident from the seventy-third psalm, throughout. But he was so overwhelmed with a view of the calamitous ſtate of God's church and people, (ſee Pſal. lxxii. 20. and read the eleven pſalms following, entitled Pſalms of Aſaph) that ſometimes (like thoſe in Iſai. xlix. 14,) he was ready to ſink under diſcouragement, as though God had quite caſt off his church and people for ever. For which he checketh himſelf, and endeavours to raiſe his hopes, from a remembrance of God's wonderful works to Iſrael of old, in bringing them out of Egypt. Pſal. lxxvii. So the Chriſtian Hebrews knew the ſincerity of their hearts, and the goodneſs of their ſtate, by the fruits of holineſs. Heb. vi. 9, 10. 11. And the confidence, that St. Paul exhorts them to hold faſt, was their confidence of the truth of Chriſtianity; for the profeſſion of which, they had already ſuffered much, and were likely to ſuffer more: and yet if they drew back, and renounced Chriſtianity, it would coſt them their ſouls. Heb. x. 23, 39.—And though it is true, our Saviour upbraided his diſciples for not believing he was riſen from the dead, of which they had ſufficient evidence, &c. yet neither they, nor any other perſon, from the beginning of Geneſis, to the end of the Revelation, were ever blamed for doubting their title to eternal life, while their evidences were not clear.

Yea, our Saviour was ſo far from encouraging his followers to this blind Faith, this bold preſumption, that his whole Sermon on the Mount is directly levelled againſt it. None are pronounced bleſſed, but thoſe who are endowed with holy and divine qualifications of heart, and lead anſwerable lives. And though men were endowed with the miraculous gifts of the holy ſpirit, and *propheſied in Chriſt's name, and in his name caſt out Devils, and did many wonderful works*, and made a great profeſſion, and had high confidence, crying, *Lord, Lord;* as our Saviour foreſaw many would: Yet if they were not under the real government of that divine temper, deſcribed in that ſermon throughout, our Saviour affirms, that at the day of Judgment he would bid them depart. Matth. vii. 21, 27.—To go on, therefore, after all this—confident we ſhall have eternal life, though unconſcious of ſanctifying operations in our own breaſts,—is,—forgive me, Theron,—is, I ſay, little better than down-right infidelity. Yea, did we believe our Saviour to be an impoſtor, we might with leſs difficulty expect to get to Heaven in ſuch a way. For as ſure as he was a Meſſenger ſent from God, ſo ſure ſhall we find the doctrine contained in his Sermon on the Mount verified at that great day, when he shall come to judge the world.—Wherefore, *be not deceived*, O my Theron! *God will not be mocked. For whatsoever a man soweth, that also shall he reap.* Gal. vi. 7.

To refer to those words of St. Paul (2 Cor. v. 7.) *We walk by Faith, and not by fight*, as you do, and to imagine, that St. Paul and the primitive Christians lived at such a low, blind, presumptuous rate, casts infinite reproach upon Christianity. For they all, with unveiled faces, *beheld as in a glass the glory of the Lord, and were changed into the same image from glory to glory, even as by the spirit of the Lord.* 2 Cor. iii. 18.—And divine and eternal things all lay open, as it were, to the Apostle's view. He looked at them; he saw them; he believed them: A sense of their infinite importance penetrated his heart. He was clean carried above all the goods and ills of this present world—and like the Sun in the firmament, he kept on a steady course, till he had finished his race, and obtained a crown of righteousness.—And thus HE *lived by Faith.* 2 Cor. iv. 16, 17, 18. and 2 Tim. iv. 6, 7, 8.—Yea, it was an avowed principle, in the Apostolic age, to judge of the goodness of their state, by the holiness of their hearts and lives. 1 Joh. iii. 6. *Whosoever abideth in him, sinneth not: Whosoever sinneth hath not seen him, neither known him.* Ver. 7. *Let no man deceive you.* Ver. 8. *He that committeth sin, is of the Devil.* Ver. 9. *Whosoever is born of God, doth not commit sin.* Ver. 10. *In this the children of God are manifest, and the children of the Devil.*—This was the Apostolic criterion: —and therefore, if any pretended to conversion, if any pretended to be acquainted with Christ, who lived not according to our Saviour's instructions, particularly in his Sermon on theMount, this was his doom; he was branded for a liar. 1 Joh. ii. 4. *He that saith, I know him, and keepeth not his commandments, is a liar, and the truth is not in him.*

Ther. I grant, the Saints in Scripture usually speak the language of assurance; but I always thought, " we had no cause to judge, that this assurance was grounded on the certainty of their own good qualifications.(1)"

Paul. Was not Abraham certain of his sincerity, when

(1). M. *p.* 184.

out of love and obedience to God he left his father's house and native country; and at one word speaking, felt a heart prepared to offer up his beloved Isaac? Was not Moses certain of his sincerity, when out of love to the cause of God, he despised all the treasures of Egypt; and afterwards felt he had rather die—had rather have his name blotted out of the book of the living, than that God should not effectually take care of the honour of his own great name? Was not Job certain of his sincerity, when with such calmness he said, *the Lord gave, and the Lord hath taken away; and blessed be the name of the Lord?* Yea, did not he constantly assert his sincerity through all his trials? Job xxxi. 1, 40. *O how love I thy law! It is my meditation all the day,* says David. Psal. cxix. 97. *Whom have I in Heaven but thee? And there is none upon earth I desire besides thee,* says Asaph. Psal. lxxiii. 25. *I have walked before thee in truth, and with a perfect heart,* says Hezekiah, looking death in the face. Isai. xxxviii. 3. *Thou knowest that I love thee,* says Peter. Joh. xxi. 17. *Our rejoicing is this, the testimony of our conscience, that in simplicity and Godly sincerity, we have had our conversation in the world,* says Paul. 2 Cor. i. 12. But why do I mention particulars? For this, even this, is the way in which all Scriptural Saints attained assurance. 1 Joh. ii. 3. *Hereby we know that we know him, if we keep his commandments.* And had you lived in the Apostolic age, O my Theron, I doubt not, all good people would have been ready, on hearing such talk as you have been too much carried away with, to cry out—*But know, thou vain man, that Faith without works, is dead.* Jam. ii: 20.

Ther. "If, in such a manner, we should acquire some little assurance, how soon may it be unsettled by the incursions of temptation, or destroyed by the insurrection of remaining sin! At such a juncture, how will it keep its standing! How retain its being! It will fare like a tottering wall before the tempest; or be *as the rush without mire, and the flag without water.* Job. viii. 11." (1)

Paul. 'Tis true, when the storm arises, the house that is built upon the sand, will be "like a tottering wall before the tempest." And "*as the rush without mire, and the flag without water,*" so the hypocrite's hope shall perish. Job viii.

(1) D. p. 362.

11, 13. But in true Saints, their Faith is "a victorious principle." *For whatsoever is born of God, overcometh the world: And this is the victory, that overcometh the world, even our Faith.* 1 Joh. v. 3. Nor shall any ever be admitted to *eat of the Tree of Life, which is in the midst of the Paradise of God,* but *he that overcometh.* This is the message which Christ, since his exaltation in Heaven, has sent to his church on Earth. Rev. ii. 7, 11, 17, 26, and iii. 5, 12, 21, and xxi. 7. And therefore, *blessed are they that do his commandments, that they may have right to the Tree of Life, and may enter in through the gates into the City.*—Rev. xxii. 14.

Ther. But are there not some, who are but *babes in Christ?*

Paul. Yes. And *as new-born babes,* they *desire the sincere milk of the word, that they may grow thereby* (1 Pet. ii. 2,) and as they grow up *unto a perfect man* (Eph. iv. 13,) their assurance increases in exact proportion. 2 Pet. i. 5, 10.

Ther. This doctrine of yours, "I fear," will wound weak Christians, and "perplex the simple minded. (1)

Paul. This doctrine, so plainly taught by Jesus Christ, and by all his Apostles, were it once thoroughly understood and firmly believed, would not only "wound" and "perplex" presumptuous hypocrites; but even slay its thousands, yea, its ten thousands: while the righteous would flourish like the green bay-tree, nourished up by such sound and good doctrine. For never did assurance, true and genuine assurance, so abound among professors, as in the Apostolic age, when this was the doctrine universally in vogue. And then the holy lives of their converts were so "exemplary, that they won the favour, and commanded the respect of all the people." And Christianity, thus adorned by the constant behaviour of its professors, gained ground every where, in spite of all the efforts of Earth and Hell. Whereas, in the days of Luther, in the days of Cromwell, and in our day, when your kind of assurance has been so much in vogue, the lives of many professors have been such as to bring reproach upon Christianity, in the sight of the world. It was this, that prejudiced the Papists against the Reformation in Luther's time. It was this, that prejudiced England against experimental religion in Cromwell's time. And it is this, it is this, O

(1) D. *p.* 361.

my Theron, that has brought vital piety into such general contempt in New England, in these late years. Our opposers cried, " Let us wait, and see how these converts will turn out a few years hence." They waited—and are confirmed in their infidelity: And thousands seem to be gone off to the Arminian scheme, or worse.—Could I speak, O my Theron, with a voice like that of the Arch-Angel, when he shall wake up all the sleeping dead, I would sound an alarm to all God's people through the Christian world, warn them against this delusion, and invite them to return back to the old Apostolic doctrine.

Ther. But, dear sir, it is not possible for me to maintain assurance in this way. To suppose that my inherent graces, which are so difficult to be discerned, at best, and so unsteady and precarious, are a proper foundation on which to build a fixed assurance, is a doctrine quite romantic.—Yea, you may as well " place the dome of a cathedral on the stalk of a tulip." (1) But on the other hand, by the witness of the spirit, in contra-distinction from inherent graces, a firm and unshaken assurance of our eternal salvation may be obtained. (2)

Paul. A firm and solid rock is this foundation; as he declares, who is the Son of God, and our final judge. No, say you, it is rather like " the stalk of a tulip !" On what evidence then will you venture your immortal soul, for a whole eternity ? On the witness of the spirit ? But, O my dear Theron, what good will this witness of the spirit do you, when you come to die ? When the storm rises, when the rain descends, the flood comes, and the wind beats upon your house, it will fall ; "like a tottering wall before the tempest," if not founded on that very rock, pointed out by our blessed Saviour. Ten thousand witnesses, from ten thousand spirits, will stand you in no stead. For as true as that Jesus was the Messiah, the man that *heareth his sayings and doth them not*, shall at last hear that dreadful word, *Depart, depart, I know you not—I know you not, ye workers of iniquity*. Then you will find, that *without holiness, no man shall see the Lord*. Heb. xii. 14. And then you will see that saying, now to you so incredible, made the test of admission into Heaven. *No man can be Christ's*

(1) *D. p.* 361.   (2) *M. p.* 184, 188.

disciple, unless he love him more than father and mother, wife and children, houses and lands, yea, more than his own life. Mat. x. 37, 38. Luk. xiv. 25, 33. You may come to the *door* and *knock*, and cry, *Lord, Lord, open to me ;* and tell him you firmly believed in your heart, you should have eternal life : But if you are found a worker of iniquity, he will bid you depart.—You may cry for mercy ; but your cries will be for ever in vain.—That spirit, O my Theron, which would make you believe your state to be good, when according to Scripture it is bad, is not the holy spirit, by which the Scriptures were inspired ; nor is its testimony to be credited.

Ther. " But if I must try the witness of the Spirit, by the sincerity of my graces, the testimony of the spirit will stand me in no stead." (1)

Paul. If you trust to the testimony of the spirit, without any regard to the sincerity of your graces, you have nothing but a spirit, a naked spirit, to depend upon. And if your spirit should prove to be Satan, transformed into an Angel of light, you are deluded—your soul is lost—for ever lost.

Ther. But if we must first know by our inherent graces, that we are the children of God, this would render the witness of the spirit needless.

Paul. Unless we first know that we have these inherent graces, we can never be assured of our good estate, according to our Saviour's Sermon on the Mount. Pray mind this, my dear Theron.

Ther. Then you deny the immediate witness of the spirit, I suppose.

Paul. This immediate witness of the spirit, which you plead for, is certainly contrary to Scripture. For, it will tell a man, his state is good, when according to God's word, it is bad. And, which is directly to the case in hand, it leads men to build their assurance, not on that rock our Saviour points out as the only safe foundation, but on something entirely different : And, I am sorry to say it, tempts men to compare what our Saviour calls a rock, to the stalk of a tulip. This spirit, therefore, being contrary to Scripture, is not the spirit of God, but the spirit of delusion.

(1) *M. p.* 188.

Ther. What then, can the witness of the spirit be?

Paul. The design of a witness is, to prove a point, to make it evident and certain; that we may believe it without the least doubt. And the proof must be legal proof, or it will not pass in law. Now, the point to be proved, is, that I am a child of God, a true disciple of Christ; and so entitled to eternal life. For, none but the children of God, and true disciples of Christ, are entitled to Heaven, according to the word of God: Which is the only rule whereby all are finally to be judged. But Christ affirms, that *no man can be his disciple, unless he love him more than father or mother, wife or children, houses or lands, yea, more than his own life:* And assures us in the most plain and express manner, that all who expect to go to Heaven, not having such hearts and lives as he describes in his Sermon, shall certainly be disappointed. If, therefore, the spirit of God means to make it evident to me, that I am a child of God, a disciple of Christ, and so an heir of Heaven, it will be, it must be, by a proof that will stand in law, a proof the Bible allows to be good. Otherwise, no credit is to be given to it: unless we will set aside this infallible law-book, by which all the Christian world is to be judged.—If the proof will not pass with our final judge, it ought not to pass with us now. But no proof will pass with our final judge, but what quadrates with the forementioned declarations of our Saviour. For he will not recede from his own words. Therefore, there is but this one way to prove to my conscience, that I am a child of God, a disciple of Christ, and so an heir of glory; there is but one thing that can possibly convince me; namely, for the spirit of God to give me such an heart as the children of God, and true disciples of Christ have, according to the plain declarations of the Gospel. By this I may know; and by nothing short of this. If this evidence is doubtful, no other can—no other should satisfy me. If this is plain, no other is necessary in order to a full assurance. Therefore, then the *spirit of God witnesseth with my spirit that I am a child of God,* when by a large communication of divine grace, this is made plain beyond all doubt. I feel the heart of a child towards God; a heart full of love, reverence, trust, obedience; a heart to go to him as a child to a father; or in other words, the spirit of adoption, whereby I cry, *Abba,*

Father. And by this I know I am a child of God. And if a child, then an heir, an heir of God, and a joint heir with Jesus Christ. Rom. viii. 16, 17, compared with verse 1, 5, 6, 9, 12, 13, 14. All true believers had *this seal of the Spirit* in the Apostolic age. Eph. i. 13. And for ought that you or I know, all true believers have had it in all succeeding ages ever since. 'Tis certain they have in some degree. And it is certain, no full assurance can be had, that is genuine and good, unless they have it in such a degree, as to be plain beyond all dispute.

Ther. I used to think the Spirit helped us immediately, not by the evidences of internal graces, but immediately, without any medium, without any evidence, to see our interest in the love of God, as held forth in the absolute unconditional grant of the Gospel. So that one might say, "pardon is mine, grace is mine, Christ and all his spiritual blessings are mine; not because I am conscious of sanctifying operations in my own breast, but because all these blessings are absolutely made over to me in the everlasting Gospel." This deed of conveyance, thus seen by the help of the spirit, was the grand demonstration of my right to pardon and salvation. And now, *believing the love that God hath unto us, we love him because he first loved us:* And so our love to God, and other graces, are a kind of secondary evidence; without any regard to which, we may, yea, previous to which, we must, have assurance by the direct act of Faith. For it is this assurance, this assurance alone, which inkindles our love and all our graces. (1)

Paul. But it has been already proved, that these blessings are not made over to us, as Sinners, absolutely and unconditionally; but only to those who are in Christ by a true and living Faith. Yours, my dear Theron, forgive me this freedom, yours is a false Gospel—a false spirit—a false Faith—a false love—all is false. Built at bottom, on no evidence "from Scripture, sense, or reason."

Ther. But amidst all this error and delusion, how shall we know the truth!

Paul. By making the written word our rule, our only rule. Once the question was, concerning Jesus of Nazareth, *art thou he that should come? Or, look we for another? Go and shew* John, said our blessed Saviour, *those things which ye*

(1) D. *p.* 358, 359, 360, 361, 362. M. *p.* 184, 188.

do hear and see. The blind receive their sight, the lame walk, and the lepers are cleansed, and the deaf hear, the dead are raised, and the poor have the Gospel preached unto them. Matth. xi. 3, 4, 5. These were the characters of the Messiah, according to the sacred writings of the old Testament; and to these he appeals. Now the question is concerning Theron, is he a true believer, a real convert, a Christian, that our Lord will own at the day of judgment? Well, go read, say I, our Saviour's Sermon on the Mount. *Blessed are the poor in spirit—blessed are they that mourn—the meek*, &c. &c. to the end. And see; Is my Theron a man of this character? If so, his house is built upon a rock: If not, it is built upon the sand. If the holy spirit has wrought so great a miracle as to make you such a man, this is what the Devil cannot do. This is such a witness of the spirit, as will pass at the great tribunal: and you will need no other. But without this, ten thousand revelations will avail you nothing. Nay, but that will be your certain doom, *I know you not, depart from me, ye workers of iniquity.*

Had one appeared, and claimed to be the Messiah, without performing those mighty works our Saviour did;—would any have been obliged to give credit to his testimony? No surely. And does a spirit come, and testify that my Theron is a child of God, without performing the mighty work of sanctification? Is Theron obliged to give credit to its witness? By no means. If the holy spirit *takes away the heart of stone, and gives you an heart of flesh; writes God's law in your heart, and puts truth in your inward part, so that you walk in his statutes and keep his commandments*—the work is done. You are a true convert. You will be saved. But without this—all is nothing.

Ther. But have not many good men had this immediate witness and testimony of the spirit, I am pleading for?

Paul. How can you know, my dear Theron, that ever there was a good man, since the foundation of the world, who had this witness? We have no instance in Scripture, nor does the word of God lead us ever to look for such a thing.

Ther. How can I know?—Strange question! When some of the best men in the world have held to the immediate witness.

K 3

DIALOGUE III.

Paul. If we do certainly know our good estate by our sanctification; is not the immediate witness needless? If men do not certainly know they are good men, by their sanctification; who on Earth can tell, but that they are hypocrites? And so, but that their immediate witness comes from the Devil? If they cannot tell—to be sure, you and I can't. Nor will their immediate witness prove the contrary; unless you can demonstrate, that Satan never transforms himself into an Angel of light. Besides, men may "hold to the immediate witness" that never had it, through some mistake. And if men have assurance by their sanctification, it is not very likely that God should make them an immediate revelation, merely to clear up a point already clear: i. e. work a kind of miracle, when there is no need of it. Besides, my dear Theron, how will you know, whether your immediate revelation comes from God, or from the Devil? Will you know by the fruits? No. For this is to "try the witness of the spirit by the sincerity of your graces." And then, as you say, "the testimony of the spirit will stand you in no stead," will be of no service. Will you know without any respect to the fruits? But how? Leave holiness out of the account, and what is there of this kind, but what the devil can do? If he can, how do you know but he will? How do you know but he does? Go to the Anabaptists in Germany, in Luther's time—go to the enthusiasts in England, in Cromwell's time, and see what the Devil has done in former ages.—Yea, I could name towns and persons in New-England, where and in whom Satan's mighty works have been to be seen, within less than twenty years ago. All the country knows, that some who appeared to have the highest confidence of a title to Heaven, have sufficiently proved to the world, that they were deluded by their immoral lives since. Will you after all, say, that it is a sin to doubt?—And that you ought to be strong in Faith, and give glory to God? Yet you must remember, that it is all, "without any evidence from Scripture, sense, or reason." And this you know! And this you own!

Who, my dear Theron—who that hath a soul to save, wou'd, with his eyes open, dare to venture his ALL for ETERNITY, on such a foundation as this! But, which is still more surprising, who, among all rational creatures, can look upon that foundation, which Christ himself calls

a rock, but as the stalk of a tulip, compared with this ! (1)
• Oh, my dear Theron, you will excuse me this freedom, this kind and well-meant freedom. A Minister of Christ ought not to flatter. Nor is it your interest to be soothed. The plain naked honest truth is what we all need to know. See with your own eyes. Judge for your own self. For your own precious immortal soul lies at stake.

As to the three questions you proposed, you have now my opinion, and the sum is this.—The true convert having, in regeneration, had his eyes open to behold the glory of God and Jesus Christ, the glory of the law and of the Gospel, he approves of the law as holy, just, and good; he believes the Gospel to be from God, acquiesces in that way of life, trusts in Christ, the great Mediator, returns home to God through him, to be forever the Lord's: and being united to Christ by Faith, he receives the holy spirit to dwell in him forever. In consequence of which, he brings forth fruit; growing in grace, and persevering therein, through all changes and trials, to the end of his life. And so, an assurance of a title to eternal life is in such sort attainable by believers, in all ordinary cases, that it must be owing to their fault, if they do not enjoy it. However, no honest man ought to believe his state to be good, with more confidence than in exact proportion to his evidence. Nor is there any evidence, that will pass with our final judge, or that ought to be of any weight with us, but real holiness. A communication of divine grace, in a large and very sensible degree, is that whereby the spirit of God makes it evident to our consciences beyond all doubt, that we are the children of God; and not by an immediate revelation.

Ther. But what do you think of the case of backsliders? May not they be in the dark about their state? And what ought they to do?

Paul. They may be in the dark, and full of doubts and fears; nor can they ever find rest to their souls, until they remember from whence they have fallen, repent and return home to God through Jesus Christ. As their departing from God is the source of all their woe; so their case

(1) *The reader may see this subject, viz. The witness of the spirit, thoroughly discussed in Mr. Edwards, on Religious Affections.*

admits of no remedy, but to repent and return to God through Jesus Christ again. It would do a backslider no good, to go to God, and say, "pardon is mine, grace is mine, Christ and all his spiritual blessings are mine." For his religion does not grow up from this belief; but from *beholding as in a glass the glory of the Lord*. But I have not time to enter upon this subject. I recommend to you Mr. Shepard, on the Parable of the Ten Virgins; in which if some expressions are not so accurate, yet on the whole, it is one of the best books I know of, for Saints under backslidings. It is so useful a book, that I wish there was one of them in every Christian family.

Here, my dear Aspasio the conversation stopt—I sat silent—I was self condemned.—Eternity all opened to my view—"I am a lost creature—Heaven pity my case"!—The tears rolled from my eyes—I could conceal my case no longer—I was persuaded Paulinus had a tender compassionate heart—therefore, I addressed him in the following manner.

Ther. Indeed, sir, I need not hear you upon the case of a backsliding Saint.—I have heard enough already—I am convinced I was never right.—I thought so before I came to see you: and all you have said has confirmed me in this opinion.—I have acted the part of a disputant; but I have done it only for light, to see what answers you would make to what might be said.—Alas! I have all to begin anew!—Just every step I have taken, is wrong. My first manifestation of the love of Christ and pardon of my sins, was wrong: the thing revealed for the truth, was a lie.—My first act of Faith was wrong: the thing believed for truth, was a lie.—My love and joy, and all my religion was wrong: only the result of self-love and delusion.—My living by Faith was wrong: It was only quieting my conscience, by holding fast my delusion.—My aversion to sanctification's being the only evidence of a good estate, was wrong: I could not stand trial by that test; and yet nothing else will pass at the great tribunal, with my final judge. But I could have no comfort this way. It tended only to doubts and fears. And doubts and fears tended to destroy all my religion.—All my religion was founded in delusion; nor was there any way for it to subsist, but to hold fast delusion, and refuse to let it go. I have been doing fo now for a long time, and had continued to do fo to my dying day, had not fome of thofe texts of Scripture you have fo often referred to, given me a fhock. And laft week I had fuch awful apprehenfions of the dreadfulnefs of eternal damnation, the amazing dreadfulnefs of going into eternity felf-deceived, as penetrated my very heart. This induced me to make you thefe vifits. And now you fee my cafe—my dreadful cafe! O dear Paulinus, be you my friend, my fpiritual guide!—What fhall I do?

Paul. How much are poor loft Sinners in this benighted world to be pitied! Generally their days—their precious days, are fpent away fecure in fin! If at any time they are a little awakened to fee their danger, how apt are they to take any way for comfort, but the right! Matth. vii. 13, 14. We are actually in fo ruined a ftate, that unlefs God interpofes, of his mere fovereign grace, and by the influences of his bleffed fpirit guides us, we fhall wander from the narrow road, get loft and perifh! Matth. xi. 25. We are enemies to God, blind to his beauty, difinclined to a reconciliation, averfe to real holinefs: and any kind of falfe religion fuits fuch depraved hearts, better than the true. Really to love God for his own infinite amiablenefs, to choofe him for our portion, to look upon fin as an infinite evil, to efteem the law, as holy, juft, and good, which requires finlefs perfection on pain of eternal damnation, and to place all our dependence on free grace through Jefus Chrift, are, of all things, moft contrary to our corrupt biaffes. Our native difinclination to the right way, renders us apt to take the wrong: and having once took it, obftinately to perfift in it. (1) Happy for you, my dear Theron, that you are brought fo far to fee your error!

(1) *Jonah* ii. 8. They that obferve lying Vanities, forfake their own mercy. *i. e. go contrary to their own intereft.* —*How often have thefe words been applied, by fome writers, to perfuade Chriftlefs Sinners to believe, that all the bleffings of the Gofpel are their own! When rather they ftand as a warning to all,* not to obferve lying Vanities, left they forfake their own mercy, *and go contrary to their own eternal intereft. Nothing being more contrary to the intereft of a poor Sinner, than to believe delufion, and fettle down on a falfe foundation.*

And for your future conduct, take these hints.——

(1) Beware you return not to that flesh-pleasing, presumptuous way of living, which had well nigh proved your ruin. Your friends may invite you back; your love of ease and present comfort, will second all their arguments, and give them ten-fold more weight than they really have.—Know it, O my Theron, there is a long eternity before you. It is worth your while to *strive to enter in at the strait gate*: Yea, to *take the kingdom of Heaven by violence*. (1) Therefore, count no self-denial, no pains, no endeavours too great; but *do with thy might, what thy hand findeth to do*.

(2) It is absolutely necessary, that you see your need of Christ, in order to come to him.—Coming to Christ, in its own nature, supposes, that we see our need of him.—You cannot see what you need Christ for, unless you see your true character and state according to law. The law is the appointed school-master, to lead Sinners to Christ. The law requires perfect obedience, on pain of eternal damnation. It requires us to love God with all our heart, as being infinitely lovely. The least defect merits eternal woe. If you take measure by this law, as your rule, your true character will appear—*dead in sin; at enmity against God, not subject to his law, neither indeed can be*.— And if you judge of your state, according to this law, you are *condemned already*, and the *wrath of God abideth on you*. you are lost—you stand guilty before God. And if the law is holy, just and good, your mouth is stopt. The Lord is *righteous when he speaketh and clear when he judgeth*, although you should perish for ever. All this you must see. Yea, you must feel it, through and through your heart, as did the Apostle Paul. *The commandment came, sin revived, and I died*. It is for want of thorough conviction, that so many awakened Sinners take up with false comfort. Their wound was never searched to the bottom.—It was skinned over too soon. And such flighty cures, though more easily performed, may prove fatal in the end. But let your legal convictions be ever so deep, you will perish, unless of his mere sovereign grace.——

(1) *Mr. Edwards's Sermons on pressing into the kingdom, and on the justice of God in the damnation of Sinners, are proper for such as Theron.*

DIALOGUE III.

(3) *He who commanded the light to shine out of darkness, shines in your heart, to give you the light of the knowledge of the glory of God, in the face of Jesus Christ.*—You are blind, quite blind, to the divine beauty. And consequently, blind to the beauty of the divine law. And so, consequently, blind too to the beauty of Christ, as dying to answer the demands of the law. And consequently under the power of unbelief. Every unregenerate man has the spirit of infidelity in his heart. 1 Joh. v. 1. Rom. x. 9. Psal. xiv. 1. You can never cordially believe, that the Son of God became incarnate, and died to answer the demands of a law, in its own nature too severe. Such a substitution cannot appear to be of God, glorious and divine; but rather shocking! You can never heartily approve of the law (which requires us to love God for his own divine excellencies, with all our hearts, on pain of eternal damnation for the least defect) as holy, just and good, unless God appears in your eyes as ONE INFINITELY LOVELY.— So depraved are you, so entirely devoid of a relish for divine beauty, that God never will appear thus amiable in your eyes, unless you are born of the spirit, have divine life immediately communicated to you from God, have a supernatural and divine sense, taste, relish, imparted to you from on high. Your heart is like the chaos; the Earth was *without form and void, and darkness was upon the face of the deep.* And dark, eternally dark, it would have been, had not God said, *Let there be light.* So unless *he who commanded the light to shine out of darkness, shines in your heart*, you will abide in eternal darkness, blind to divine beauty; to the glories of God and Christ, of Law and Gospel. And if the Gospel continues thus hid from you, you are lost, forever lost. 2 Cor. iv. 3, 6.

If the divine law, in itself, is not holy, just and good, Christ's dying to answer its demands cannot make it so.— If the law was too severe, Christ's death was a most shocking affair! A dislike of the divine law, as too rigorous, is the root of all the chief errors in the Christian world; yea, it is the root of the prevailing infidelity of the present age. And it now lies at the bottom of all your hard thoughts of God, O my Theron; which the Devil is not the author of, as some imagine, in such cases. And is a mighty bar to your believing in Christ. And nothing can effectually remove it, but divine light, imparted in regeneration. (1)

(4) Bid a final adieu to vain and carnal companions, to all sinful and carnal pleasures and pastimes, and to every known sin; all which tend to stupify the heart. And by reading, meditation, and prayer, endeavour with all your might to obtain a realizing sense of your true character and state. Cast yourself at the foot of sovereign grace, and cry, with the blind man, *Lord, that I might receive my sight!* "That I may see and know what I am, what I deserve, what I need; and the only way to obtain relief, by free grace through Jesus Christ." However, that you may not trust in your own doings to recommend you to the divine favour, nor be encouraged from your own goodness to hope for mercy, constantly remember——

(1) *No man can understandingly and heartily look to, trust in, or depend upon the mediation of Christ, unless he sees his need of him as a mediator. No man can see his need of the mediation of Christ, unless he sees that which renders his mediation needful. Now the goodness and excellency of the divine law, which we have broke, is the only thing which originally rendered the mediation of Christ needful. But for this, the Sinner might have been saved without a mediator, without an atonement, as well as with. Nay, better. For if the law were too severe, it had evidently been more honourable for God to have repealed, or abated it, than to have appointed his Son to answer its demands in our stead.*

Some seem to think, that the law, although suited to the strength of man before the fall, and so a good law for an innocent, holy creature, yet is too rigorous for a fallen world. And therefore imagine, that Christ died to purchase an abatement, and to bring it down to a level with our present weakness.— But if the law was too severe, the justice of the divine nature would have moved the governor of the world to have made all proper abatements; nor was the death of Christ needful in the case. Surely Christ need not die, merely to get justice done us.

Some seem to look upon God the Father, as all made up of wrath, the Sinner's enemy: And on God the Son, as all made up of love, the Sinner's friend. And imagine, he died to assuage his Father's anger, and move his compassions towards poor Sinners. And so they love Christ, while they hate God and his law.—But this is all a mere chimera. The Father

(5) That the divine law, which you are under, requires that you love GOD for himself; whereas, all you do is merely from self-love. Yea, it requires you to love God with all your heart; whereas, there is no love to God in your heart. And it requires this sinless perfection on pain of eternal damnation, for the least defect; so that by the law you are already condemned. By mere law you are therefore absolutely and forever undone. You stand guilty before God.—But mere law is the rule of right, and standard of justice. If justice should take place, you then see your doom. There is no hope from this quarter.— Wherefore you lie at the mercy of God, his mere mercy, who is absolutely unobliged to grant you any relief, for any thing you can do. He might justly have left all mankind in this state, without a Saviour. And he may, on the same grounds, as justly leave you in this state, without a Sanctifier. He did not give his Son to save this lost world, for our righteousness sake: Yea, had we been righteous, we should not have needed his Son to die in our stead.— Nor does God give his holy spirit, to convert any poor perishing Sinner, for his righteousness sake: Yea, it is his being entirely destitute of all that is spiritually good, and

is as full of love and goodness, as the Son. The Son is as holy and just, as great a friend to the law, and as great an enemy to sin, as the Father. They are both of one heart. Yea, they are both one God. Job. x. 30.

Some seem to resolve the whole of God's law and government, and the death of Christ, into the mere arbitrary will of God: As though the whole were not the result of wisdom, of infinite wisdom, but rather of mere arbitrary will. But it does not appear, by Scripture or otherwise, that the infinitely wise God ever determines any thing without reason, or does any thing but what is wise for him to do. But rather the whole of divine revelation joins to confirm the truth of St. Paul's observation, that God worketh all things after the COUNSEL of his own will. Eph. i. 11. *All his perfections, if I may so speak, sit in council: And all his decrees and works are the result of infinite holiness, justice and goodness, directed by infinite wisdom.*

There is but one way to solve the difficulty. There is but one thing can ever satisfy our hearts. A sight of the glory of

L

dead in sin, that occasions his standing in perishing need of converting grace. And although all the promises of God are in Christ Jesus, *Yea, and in him amen;* yet, as to those who are out of Christ, they are so far from being entitled to the promises, that *the wrath of God abideth on them.*—Therefore——

(6) If ever you are *renewed by the holy Ghost*, it will be, not for any goodness in you, but merely from God's self-moving mercy, and sovereign grace, through Jesus Christ, Tit. iii. 5, 6.

(7) How dreadful soever this representation makes your case appear; yet, if this is your true state, you must see it, that you may know your need of Christ and free grace, and be in a capacity, understandingly, to give a proper reception to the glad tidings of the Gospel, viz. That through Christ, God is ready to be reconciled to the returning penitent, who justifies God, approves his law, quits all claims, and looks only to free grace, through Jesus Christ, for salvation. Luk. xviii. 13. Rom. iii. 24, 25, 26.

(8) Saving Faith consists in looking to free grace, through Jesus Christ, for salvation; thus viewing God's law, and your own case, as they really be. And he that thus *believeth, shall be saved.* Therefore, *repent and be converted, and your sins shall be blotted out. Behold, now is the accepted time, and now is the day of salvation!* And by me, one of Christ's ministers, *God does beseech you to be re-*

the God of glory, will open to view the grounds and reasons of the law, and convince us that it is holy, just and good, glorious and amiable, and worthy to be kept in credit, to be magnified and made honourable, by the obedience and death of the Son of God.—But then if the law is good, we who have broke it, are not fit to live. Death is our due. The Judge of all the Earth cannot but do right. His nature, law and honour, call aloud for our destruction. He cannot be just, if he don't destroy us. It will bring everlasting reproach upon his government, to spare us, considered merely as in ourselves. When this is felt in our hearts, then, and not till then, shall we feel our need of Christ, and be prepared to look to the free *grace of God thro' the redemption that is in Christ, and to exercise* Faith *in his* blood, who was set forth to be a propitiation, to declare God's righteousness, that he might be just, and yet the justifier of him that believeth in Jesus.

conciled, and I pray you in Chrift's ftead, be you reconciled to God. For God hath made his only begotten Son to be a facrifice for fin, that all who are united to him by a true and living Faith, might return to God with acceptance, and be juftified, and have eternal life through him.

Ther. Every word you have fpoken, finks down into my ears. The Lord grant, the truth may pierce my heart through and through.—The reft of my days I will devote to the bufinefs of my foul.—I thank you for your kind inftructions—I beg your prayers—the anguifh of my heart calls me to retire—Adieu!—dear fir, Adieu!

Paul. May the only wife God be your effectual inftructor, my Theron!—Adieu!

To my dear Afpafio,

Thefe Dialogues are prefented by

YOUR AFFECTIONATE

THERON.

LETTER II.

THERON TO ASPASIO.

New-England, March 12, 1759.

DEAR ASPASIO,

MY melancholy Letter of December laſt, with a copy of the ſubſtance of the converſation I had with Paulinus, at three ſeveral times, you have doubtleſs received long ago, as it is now three months ſince I wrote. If you have been impatient at hearing nothing from your friend for ſo long a time, I more:—toſſed to and fro, for months together, like a feeble ſhip at ſea, in a tempeſtuous night, ready every moment to ſink.

At firſt (I mean after I had left Paulinus, and retired, as I had determined to ſpend much time in meditation and prayer) I called in queſtion a maxim, he ſeemed to take for granted; that "we are all, by nature, under a law, requiring perfect obedience, on pain of eternal damnation": Which he ſo inſiſted was a glorious law, holy, juſt and good.—Thus I thought with myſelf—"Perfect obedience! That is more than we can yield.—And am I for ever loſt for the firſt offence?—How can that be juſt! Can the kind Father of the univerſe, require more of his creature, MAN, than he can do? And then puniſh him with eternal damnation, for not doing!—Can this be right?" Indeed I now felt I had an Arminian heart.

But on a certain evening, as I was reading Saint Paul's Epiſtle to the Romans and Galatians, in which he affirms, that *the wrath of God is revealed from Heaven againſt all ungodlineſs and unrighteouſneſs of men*; that the very Heathen themſelves *are without excuſe*; that *the whole world ſtand guilty before God, and every mouth ſtopt*; that the law *curseth every man who continueth not in all things written in the book of the law, to do them;* and that Chrift was made a curfe for us, to redeem us from the curfe of that very law; I was greatly fhocked and confounded. One while I faid, this law cannot be right." But again, I faid, " why then was it not repealed? Why did the Son of God bear its curfe, and die to anfwer its demands?" I looked through the Old Teftament, I looked through the New; and this notion of the law, I faw was fo inwrought into both, that it muft be granted; or the whole of divine Revelation given up.—I felt the heart of an infidel—I was full of doubts and' fcruples as to the truth of the Bible. And when I reflected on the external evidence of divine Revelation, as reprefented by our late writers, particularly by Doctor Leland, whofe view of Deiftical Writers, I had lately read, I was drove even to Atheifm. For if there is a God, the Bible muft be true. But if the Bible is true, the law in all its rigour, is holy, juft, and good.

Thus I was unfettled in all my principles, and fet afloat as on a boifterous ocean, like a fhip without a compafs or an helm; in great anxiety and deep perplexity, ready many times to conclude to go back, at all adventures, to my old hope, as the only way for reft : thinking, I had as good live and die on a falfe-hope, as live and die in defpair.

Till on a certain time, I began thus to reafon in my heart:—" whence all thefe doubts, O my foul! Whence all thefe Arminian, Socinian, deiftical, atheiftical thoughts! Whence have they all arifen! From viewing the law of God, as *requiring perfect obedience, on pain of eternal damnation*—But why? Had I rather turn an Infidel, than approve the law as holy, juft, and good?—Is this my heart! Once I thought I loved God, and loved his law, and loved the Gofpel.—Where am I now!" Thefe words of the Apoftle feemed to picture my very cafe; *The carnal mind is enmity againft God, and is not fubject to his law, neither indeed can be.* Rom. viii. 7. This text engaged my attention, and fixed my thoughts. And looking into my heart, more and more, I found the fpirit of an enemy to God and to his law, in full poffeffion of my foul.

Till now I had entertained, at leaft fometimes, a fecret hope, that my ftate was good; although it feemed as if I had quite given it up. But now I began in a new manner to fee, or rather to feel, I was dead in fin.

A realizing sense of God, as the infinitely great Being, the almighty Governor of the world, holy, and just, a sin-revenging God, a consuming fire against the workers of iniquity, daily grew upon my heart, and set home the law, in all its rigour. A fresh view of all my evil ways from my youth up, continually prayed upon my spirits—Eternity! Eternity!—Oh how dreadful it seemed! I watched, I prayed, I fasted—I spared no pains to obtain an humble, broken, contrite heart. But notwithstanding my greatest efforts, my heart grew worse—my case more desperate: till in the issue, I found myself absolutely without strength—dead in sin—lost—condemned by law—self-condemned—my mouth stopt—guilty before God—I was forced to be silent; as it was but fair and right, that God should be an enemy to me, who was an enemy to him; and but just, if he should forever cast me off. And in this case I had perished, had not mere sovereign grace interposed. But in the midst of this midnight-darkness, when all hope seemed to be gone, at a moment when I least expected relief (for, *the commandment came, sin revived, and I died*) even now, God, *who commanded the light to shine out of darkness, shined in my heart.* —Thus was the case.

It was in the evening (after the day had been spent in fasting and prayer) as I was walking in a neighbouring grove, my thoughts fixed with the utmost attention, on God, as a consuming fire against his obstinate enemies—on the law, as cursing the man that continueth not in all things written therein to do them—on my whole life, as one continued series of rebellion—on my heart, as not only dead to God, and to all good, but full of enmity against the divine law and government, and (shocking to remember!) full of enmity against God himself. Feeling that my whole heart was thus dead in Sin, and contrary to God, I felt it was a gone case with me: There was no hope—no, not the least, from any good in me, or ever to be expected from me. I lay at God's mercy, forfeited—justly condemned, lost—helpless—undone! And *I will have mercy, on whom I will have mercy*, I clearly saw, was the fixed resolution of the Almighty. Thus stood my case—a poor, wretched, sinful, guilty creature, completely ruined in myself! I retired to the most remote part of the grove. Where, hid under the darkness of the evening, and the shade of spreading trees, no eye could see me. First, I smote on my breast; but could not look up to Heaven, nor speak one word. I fell on my knees: But I could not speak. I fell prostrate on the ground: And felt as one ready to sink into eternal ruin. Having no hope, unless from the sovereign good pleasure of my angry Judge. As I lay prostrate on the ground, a new scene gradually opened to my view. It was new, and it was exceeding glorious!— God appeared not only infinitely great, and infinitely holy, as the SOVEREIGN of the whole UNIVERSE; but also infinitely glorious: even so glorious, as to be worthy of all the love and honour, which his law requires. The law appeared holy, just, and good: I could not but approve it, from my very heart: and said within myself, ere I was aware, "Let all Heaven for ever love and adore the infinitely glorious MAJESTY, although I receive my just desert, and perish for ever!" Next came into view, the whole Gospel-way of life, by free grace through Jesus Christ; the wisdom, glory and beauty of which, cannot be expressed. The law did bear the divine image, and was glorious; but the Gospel exhibited all the divine perfections in a still brighter manner. and far exceeded in glory. I saw, God might, consistently with his honour, in this way, receive the returning Sinner, however ill-deserving. I saw he was ready to do it—that all might come —even the vilest and the worst, encouraged by the selfmoving goodness and boundless grace of God, and the mediation, merits and atonement of Christ; I looked up to God through Jesus Christ for mercy, and through Jesus Christ, gave up myself to the Lord, to be for ever his, to love him and live to him for ever.—Here prostrate on the ground, I thus lay above an hour, contemplating the ineffable glories of God, the beauty of his law, and the superabundant excellency of the Gospel-way of life, by free grace through Jesus Christ: I believed the Gospel, I trusted in Christ, and gave up myself to God through him, to be for ever his, with a pleasure divinely sweet, infinitely preferable to the most agreeable sensations I had ever before experienced. What I enjoyed this hour, did more, unspeakably more, than over-balance all the distresses of months past. (1) To relate how I spent the night, and

---

(1) *Theron's Narrative of his former supposed conversion (Let. I.) and of his experiences (here) is not designed to*

how I have spent my days and nights ever since, I shall omit. But you shall soon hear again, my dear Aspasio, from

YOUR AFFECTIONATE

THERON.

suggest, that either false or true converts all experience things, in every circumstance, just alike: but only to point out the general nature of these two kinds of conversion, in a manner so familiar, that the weakest Christian may see the difference.— And if any Christian cannot recollect so exactly the particulars of his first conversion, yet as all after-acts of grace are of the same nature with the first, a clear understanding of the true nature of saving grace, may help him to discern his true state.

N. B. What is the true nature of saving grace, is not to be decided by the experiences of this or that man, or party of men: but only by the word of God.

LETTER III.

THERON TO ASPASIO.

New-England, April 2, 1759.

DEAR ASPASIO,

WITH pleasure I now again sit down to write to my distant friend, and send my heart beyond the Atlantic to my Aspasio.—For neither time, nor place, nor any change can wipe your memory from my mind.

Methinks, were I now with you, as once at the house, the hospitable house, of the wealthy and illustrious Philenor, I would tell you all my heart. I remember how you urged me to believe; and how I longed to find some safe foundation, some sure evidence, on which to build my Faith; and with Thomas, to cry, *my Lord, my God!*— Now I have found it! I have found it!—*I believe, that Jesus is the Christ.* 1 Joh. v. 1. I believe, that *God hath set him forth to be a propitiation—to declare his righteousness—that he might be just, and the justifier of him which believeth in Jesus.* Rom.

iii. 25, 26. I *believe, that God raifed him from the dead.* Rom. x. 9. I believe, that *Chrift is entered into Heaven, now to appear in the prefence of God,* as the Jewiſh high-prieſt of old entered into the holy of holies on the day of atonement, (Heb. ix. 24.) and that he is *the way to the Father,* (Joh. xiv. 6.) the *door, by whom men enter in.* Joh. x. 9. And that *whofoever will, may come* to God through him. Rev. xxii. 17.—Wherefore I am emboldened to *enter into the holieft by the blood of Jefus,* even into the very pre-fence of the *thrice holy* ONE *of Ifrael,* in whofe fight *the Heavens are not clean* ; and to come to God in *full affurance of Faith, nothing doubting* but that God is as willing to be reconciled through Chriſt, as the Father was to receive the returning prodigal ; and as ready to *give his holy fpirit to them that afk him,* as ever parent was to give bread to an hungry child. Heb. x. 19, 22. Mat. vii. 11.—*For he that fpared not his own Son, but delivered him up for us all, how fhall he not with him alfo freely give us all things ;* if we accept his Son as he is offered, and come to God through him, for all things, as we are invited ? Rom. viii. 32. Joh. i. 12 and xvi. 23.—For, God's honour is fafe, God's law is anfwered, God's juſtice is fatisfied ; and all my guilt, infinite as it is, is no bar in the way of my reception into the divine favour ; free as his infinite grace, felf-moving as his boundless goodnefs is, and appears to be, by the gift of his Son.

This way of falvation, my dear Afpafio, is glorious for God, fafe for the Sinner, effectual to promote holinefs, even *the power of God to falvation, to every one that believeth :* And if the Gofpel is true there is no room to doubt. " For we are conſtrained to believe on the cleareſt evidence."— Yea, " our affurance is impreffed" by complete demon-ſtration.

'Tis glorious for God.—For God's law and authority are as much honoured, as if the whole world had been damned : And his grace more glorified, than if Man had never fell.—An incarnate God upon the crofs, in the room of a rebellious world, fets God's infinite hatred of fin, his inflexible refolution to punish it, and the infinite goodnefs of his nature, in a light, infinitely clear, infinitely bright. And contains a fund of inſtruction, which never can be exhauſted, by angels and faints, throughout the endlefs ages of eternity.—The more I think, the more I am fwallowed up! confounded! overwhelmed! O! *the height, the depth, the length, the breadth, of the love of God, which passeth all understanding*—O! *the depth of the riches of the wisdom and knowledge of God.* The creation of the Universe was a great work: It caused the Eternal power and Godhead of the Creator clearly to be seen: But compared to the incarnation and death of the Son of God, the Creator, it is not to be mentioned, nor is it worthy to come into mind. Even the application of Chrift's redemption, in the latter day, is a more glorious work than the first creation of the world. Isai. lxv. 17. *Behold, I create new Heavens, and a new Earth: and the former shall not be remembered, nor come into mind.*—Indeed, it had been but a small thing, for the Creator, by his Almighty word, to have called millions of such systems as ours into being—a thing not worthy to be noticed—nay, scarce worth one single thought—compared with—with what?—Let all nature tremble at the news—The incarnation, and the death of the ALMIGHTY CREATOR, in the room of his rebel-creatures, that the honour of his Father's law and government might be effectually secured, while sovereign infinite grace interposes to save the self-ruined, hell-deserving rebels, to the eternal disappointment of Satan, God's enemy, and our mortal foe!

And can it now, after all this, be a question, whether God is ready to be reconciled to those, who, on his own invitation, return to him through Jesus Chrift? Or can it be a question, whether Chrift is willing to be their Mediator and High-prieft, in the court of Heaven, in the holy of holies above?—What! after God has given his Son to die, that confiftently with his honour he might receive such to favour—he not willing! Infinitely incredible!—What! after the Son of God has left his Father's bosom, to lie in a manger! to groan in the garden! And, *be astonished, O ye Heavens, and be ye horribly afraid!*—To hang and die upon the crofs, in the room of a God-hating, Chrift-murdering world; that he might honour his Father's law, break up Satan's plot, and open a way for the Sinner's return! Yet he not willing!—What! willing to die on the crofs, and not willing to mediate in Heaven! Infinitely incredible! Yea, if possible, more than infinitely incredible!—So certain my dear Aspasio, as the Gofpel is true, just so certain may your Theron be, that God is ready to be reconciled to the Sinner, who returns to him through Jesus Christ. Nor does he need a new revelation in the case: nor does he need to be assured of any proposition not plainly revealed in the Gospel. Enough has been already DONE! enough has been already SAID!—But never did your Theron believe these things with all his heart, till by seeing the glory of the God of glory, he saw the grounds and reasons of the law, pronounced it holy, just and good, and worthy to be magnified and made honourable, even by the death of GOD'S OWN SON. 1 Joh. v. 1.

And this kind of Faith, in the nature of things, cannot be without works. For, while your Theron, through the influences of the holy spirit, doth *with open face, behold as in a glass the glory of the Lord;* what can he do, but love, admire, adore the God of glory; and give up himself forever to him through Jesus Christ?—And now—*how can we that are dead to sin, live any longer therein?* We are *crucified with Christ—buried with him—risen with him*—and can sin, after all, *have dominion over us!* Impossible. Rom. vi. 2. 14. The gratitude, the ingenuity of unrenewed nature, I grant, is not to be depended upon. *Israel sang God's praise but soon forgot his works.* But *beholding as in a glass the glory of the Lord,* from day to day through the course of our lives, *we are,* we cannot but be, *changed into the same image from glory to glory, even as by the spirit of the Lord.* 2 Cor. iii. 18.

And, believing the Gospel to be true, no doubt remains, of the safety of our returning to God through Jesus Christ. His glory and beauty inclines me to return. His grace through Christ puts courage in my heart. I return. I find rest to my weary soul. And by this I know, my " Faith is real, and no delusion," even *because he hath given me of his spirit,* (1 Joh. iv. 13.) set his seal upon my heart (Eph. i. 13.) made me his child, in the very temper of my soul (Rom. viii. 16.) and *in my heart his law is written, and in his ways I love to walk.* Ezek. xxxvi. 26, 27. But as to this, Heaven forbid! that your Theron's confidence should ever be greater than his evidence; his evidence, not only now, but in all future times.——I am, forever,

YOUR AFFECTIONATE

THERON.

LETTER IV.

THERON TO ASPASIO.

New-England, April 3, 1759.

DEAR ASPASIO,

MANY an agreeable hour have we wandered over all the works Nature; viewed the Heavens above, the Earth beneath, and surveyed the mighty Ocean; nor did you ever fail to intermingle devout reflections. If now instead of painting the beauties of the Creation, we rise at once to contemplate the glories of the CREATOR, glories infinitely superior to those of fields and forests, gardens and palaces; yea, infinitely superior to the bright expance of Heaven, adorned with all its shining orbs—no theme can my Aspasio better please.

GOD! how awful is the name! how great is the Being! *Behold, the nations are as a drop of the bucket, and are counted as the small dust of the balance: Yea, all nations before him are as nothing, and they are counted to him less than nothing, and vanity.* And so great is the excellency of the DIVINE MAJESTY, so exceeding great is his beauty; that to behold his glory, and love and honour and enjoy him, is Heaven itself: It is the chief happiness of all that world. The Seraphim, while he sitteth on his throne, high and lifted up, as the great MONARCH of the Universe, through the brightness of his glory, cover their faces, unable to behold: and, as in a perfect extasy, cry, *holy, holy, holy!*— This is his character, the character he exemplifies in all his conduct, as Lord of Hosts, as governor of the world; in a view of which, they add, *the whole Earth is full of his glory.* Isai. vi. 3.

The two grandest affairs, which, according to Scripture, ever have been, or ever will be, transacted in the govern-

ment of this glorious monarch, are the work of our RE-
DEMPTION by the death of his Son, and the final JUDG-
MENT of the world. These, therefore, let us contemplate,
that in them we may behold, *as in a glass, the glory of the
LORD.*

Who was his Son? *The brightness of his glory, and the
image of his person: By whom, and for whom, all things
were created.* Loved equally to himself, and honoured
with equal honours in all the world above. Let us view
him on the Cross, incarnate! View him there as an incarnate God, dying for Sinners! And fix our attention,
whole hours together, on this greatest, and most wonderful of all God's works! The plan was laid in Heaven.—
This great event was *determined in the council* there. Act.
iv. 28. All the perfections of the Godhead sat in council,
when it was decreed, the Son of God should die.—Strange
decree! Why was it made?—Astonishing! Why did it
ever come to pass?—Did he die, to move the compassions
of his almighty Father towards a rebellious race? No:
For, to give his Son thus to die, was greater grace, than at
one sovereign stroke to have cancelled all our debt, and
pardoned all the world. Did he die, to take away or les-
sen the evil nature and ill-desert of sin? No: For infinite
purity and impartial justice must look upon the rebellions
of a revolted world, as odious and ill-deserving, as if he
had not died. He died, to bear the punishment due to us.
We were under the curse; he was made a curse in our
room; *set forth to be a propitiation,* by his holy Father, *to
declare his righteousness,* and shew the rectitude of his government in the eyes of all created intelligences; *that he
might be just,* do as his law threatens, and yet not *damn,
but justify the Sinner that believeth in Jesus.*

Eternal damnation was our due, according to the divine
law: a law not founded in arbitrary will. A law, arbitrarily made, may be arbitrarily repealed; but a law only
declaring what is fit, must forever stand in force. To rise
in rebellion against the infinitely glorious majesty of Heaven, deserved eternal damnation; as he is infinitely worthy
of the highest love and honour from all his intelligent creatures. His infinite amiableness and honourableness infinitely oblige us to love and honour him. All our heart
and mind and strength are his due. The least defect de-

M

fect deserves eternal woe. Thus the Omniscient viewed the case.—His Son, in the same view, approved the law as strictly just. Both looked on the sacrifice and death of an incarnate God, in the room of Sinners, to open a way for their salvation, as a plan infinitely preferable to the law's repeal by a sovereign act. The Son had rather endure the most painful, shameful death, than that one tittle of the law should fail; it was so strictly just.—God ought to have his due——The law barely asserts the rights of the Godhead. So much, however, was his due, as to be loved with all the heart, and obeyed in every thing. And so worthy was the Deity of this love and obedience, that the least defect deserved eternal death. " 'Tis right, 'tis right," said the eternal Son, " that the first instance, or the least degree of disrespect to my eternal Father, should incur eternal ruin to the sinning creature. And I had rather become incarnate and die myself, than yield this point." That God is infinitely amiable—that he ought to be loved with all our heart—that the infinite excellency of his nature infinitely obliges us—can never be set in a stronger light, than it is by the cross of CHRIST.

The infinite dignity of the Mediator, and the extreme sufferings he underwent, as an equivalent to our eternal woe, in the loudest manner proclaim, that the law was just —just in the eyes of God—and just in the eyes of his Son. A law, threatening eternal damnation, infinite goodness would never have enacted, had not impartial justice called for it. Much less would infinite goodness have appointed God's own Son to answer its demands, if in its own nature too severe. To suppose, the Son of God died to answer the demands of a law, in its own nature, cruel, is to make God a tyrant, and the death of his Son the most shocking affair that ever happened!

But what did this law, of which we so often speak, require? Say, my dear Aspasio, what was the first and chief command? Your master's answer you approve—*Thou shalt love the Lord thy God with all thy heart*. But why was love required? Because God was lovely. And why the penalty so great? Because his loveliness was infinite. If the infinite amiableness of the divine Being does not lay an infinite obligation on his creatures, to love him for being what he is, how can we justify the law's demands, or vindicate the wisdom of God in the death of his Son?

From the cross, where an incarnate God asserted the rights of the Godhead by his dying pains, let us pass to the awful tribunal; where the same incarnate God, arrayed in all his Father's glory, with all the Hosts of Heaven in his train, by the last sentence, which he will pronounce upon his Father's enemies, dooming them to the burning lake, to welter for eternal ages in woe, will still proclaim the justice of the law: Would infinite goodness, would our compassionate Saviour, would he who wept over Jerusalem, the kind and tender-hearted Jesus, love to pronounce a sentence so infinitely dreadful, if it were not strictly just? Yet he will do it, without the least reluctance; yea, with the highest pleasure: while Angels and Saints shout forth their hallelujah's, all around him.

But can this ever be accounted for, on any other hypothesis, than that the infinitely glorious MONARCH of the universe appears, clearly appears, in that solemn hour, to be infinitely worthy of all that love and honour his law required, in being what he is; and so sin an infinite evil?

If sin is really an infinite evil, then it is meet that it should be discountenanced and punished as such, i. e. with an infinite punishment, i. e. with the eternal pains of Hell. And it was fit, that the governor of the world should make a law, thus to punish it. And fit, that this law should be magnified and made honorable. And even wise, in the eyes of infinite wisdom, that one by nature GOD, should become incarnate, and die in the Sinner's stead, rather than set the law aside. And on this hypothesis, the final doom of the wicked may well appear perfectly beautiful in the eyes of all holy intelligences. But sin cannot be an infinite evil, unless we are under infinite obligations to do otherwise.

LOVE is the thing required. Not merely a love of gratitude to God, as an almighty benefactor: but a love of esteem, complacence and delight. We may feel grateful to a benefactor, merely as such, without even a knowledge of his general character; yea, when his general character would not suit us, did we know it? The Israelites, notwithstanding their joy and gratitude at the side of the Red-Sea, were far from a disposition to be suited, to be pleased, to be enamoured, with such a being as GOD was. Yea, the more they knew of him, the less they seemed to like him; so that in less than two years they were for going back to Egypt again. But if we may feel grateful towards God, merely as our almighty benefactor, without the knowledge of his true character; yet esteem, complacence and delight, suppose his true character known; as that is the object of this kind of love. And what can lay us under infinite obligations to love God, in this sense, but his own infinite AMIABLENESS? Yet the divine law requires us to love God with this kind of love—and that with all our hearts, on pain of eternal damnation for the least defect. And this law was binding on all mankind, previously to a consideration of the gift of Christ to be a Saviour.

While, therefore, the law supposes our obligations to be infinite; and the death of the Son of God, and the final judgment, give the highest possible proof, that the OMNISCIENT esteems the law exactly right; the infinite dignity, excellency and glory of the MOST HIGH GOD, is hereby set in the strongest point of light.

Take away the infinite amiableness of the Deity, and we, in effect, unged him.—He ceases to be the GOD OF GLORY—He ceases to be a proper object of this supreme regard, in the eyes of finite intelligences—It is no longer an infinite evil, not to love him—The law is no longer just —The death of Christ is needless—And the whole system of doctrines revealed in the Bible, is sapped at the foundation—Nothing remains, to a thinking man, but infidelity.

And yet, dear Aspasio, this was my very case. The infinite amiableness of the Deity, which is the real foundation of all true religion, was wholly left out of the account, in my love and joy, and in all my religious affections. All my love and joy and zeal arose from my Faith. And my Faith consisted but in believing that Christ, pardon and Heaven were mine.—I rejoiced just like the graceless Israelites, in a sense of their great deliverance, and in expectation of soon arriving to the promised land, a land *flowing with milk and honey, the glory of all lands*. Their's was a graceless, selfish joy; and so was mine.— Their's was soon over; and so was mine. Their carcases finally fell in the wilderness; and, but for the sovereign grace of God, this also had been my very case.

Oh! my dear Aspasio, whose entertaining pen gains the attention of thousands on both sides the Atlantic, pity the ignorance of benighted souls, and guard them against the dangers, which had well nigh proved the ruin of your own pupil.

YOUR AFFECTIONATE

THERON.

LETTER V.

THERON TO ASPASIO.

New-England, April 4, 1759.

MY DEAR ASPASIO,

WHILE I view God the Creator, whose almighty word gave existence to the whole system—while I view him as the original author and sole proprietor of the whole universe; whose are all things in Heaven and Earth; I see, the right of government naturally belongs to him. It is meet, that he should be KING in his own world: And he cannot but have a rightful authority over the works of his own hands.—While I view him as moral governor of the world, seated at the head of the intelligent creation, *on a throne high and lifted up*, Heaven and Earth *filled with his glory*, as the THRICE HOLY ONE; and hear him utter his voice, saying, I AM THE LORD, and, BESIDES ME THERE IS NO OTHER GOD; and hear him command all the world to *love and adore and obey him, on pain of eternal damnation;* a spirit of love to his glorious majesty inspires me with joy, and makes me exult, to see him thus exalted, and thus honoured. I love to hear him proclaim his law, a law *holy, just and good,* glorious and amiable. I am glad with all my heart, the almighty Monarch of the universe is so engaged, that all his subjects *give unto God the glory due unto his name.* Psal. xcvi. 8.

His law, his glorious law, which once, enemy to God that I was, appeared like "the laws of Draco," now shines with a beauty all divine. I had almost said, it is *the brightness of his glory, and the express image of his person.*—For indeed it is an exact transcript of his glorious perfections, the very picture of his heart, HOLY, JUST, and GOOD. Rom. vii. 12.

When the God of glory dwelt in the Jewish temple, in the pillar of cloud, over the mercy-seat, his law was by his special command deposited in the Ark, the very holiest place in the holy of holies, as the dearest, choicest treasure. Thus was it done to the law, which God delighted to honour. But this honour, great as it was, is not to be mentioned, nor is it worthy to come into mind, since that infinitely greater regard to the divine law, which God has shewn in the gift of his SON. An incarnate God on the cross, has *magnified the law, and made it honourable,* beyond, infinitely beyond, what was ever done before. But all this honour, infinitely great as it was, was but just equal to what the law deserved.

While I view God, my Creator, my rightful Lord and owner, my sovereign king, the GOD OF GLORY; and see his infinite worthiness of supreme love and honour; I feel, that the least disrespect to his glorious Majesty is an infinite evil. I pronounce the law in all its rigour, *holy, just and good.* Even as a *ministration of death and condemnation, it appears glorious,* (2 Cor. iii. 7, 8.) and I heartily acquiesce in the equity of the sentence, with application to myself. This makes me feel my need of CHRIST, and prepares my heart to return home to God, forever to live to him. *For I through the law am dead to the law, that I might live unto God.* Gal. ii. 19.

The law, my dear Aspasio, threatens eternal damnation for the very first transgression, for even the least defect. Gal. iii. 10. I break the law every moment; and therefore every moment I merit eternal woe: Such an infinite evil is sin. It appeared glorious in the eyes of GOD, thus to punish sin, when he made his law—It appeared glorious in the eyes of CHRIST, that sin should be thus punished, when he went as a lamb to the altar, and voluntarily stretched himself upon the cross to die in the Sinner's room. And in a clear view of the glory of the GOD OF GLORY. I see the grounds and reasons of the law; it is *holy, just and good.*—I see why Christ was so willing to be nailed to the cross in the Sinner's stead; *to magnify the law and make it honourable.* And I *have fellowship,* a fellow-feeling, *with Christ in his sufferings;* and in the temper of my heart, am *made conformable to his death.* Phil. iii. 10. I feel towards God, and law, and sin, in a measure, as he did. Or, to express all my heart in one emphatical phrase, I AM CRUCIFIED WITH CHRIST. Gal. ii. 20. " The law is good, I deserve to die. I lay my neck upon the block, or rather stretch my hands upon the cross: and say, the *law is holy, just and good,* and cry, AMEN, AMEN, AMEN, twelve times going: "—as God, of old, taught his church to do. Deut. xxvi. 14, 20. (1)

(1) *I must confess, my dear Aspasio, I am shocked, to hear some Divines represent the law as a tyrant, as tyrannizing over Christ upon the cross, as tyrannizing over Sinners, as being slain for its tyranny, &c. For these hard speeches are not so much against the law, as against the God that made it. Just as if God and his law were tyrants, while Christ and his Gospel are all made up of* LOVE! *But shocking as this is, yet I must own, this was once the very temper of my heart. (See the Marrow of Mod. Div. with Notes. p.* 146.)—*I loved the Gospel: I did not love the law. The dying love of Christ, O, how sweet a theme! Law, obligation, duty, were disagreeable, dead, and legal things. Faith, pardon, joy, Heaven, Grace, free Grace, these topics only ravished my heart. Christ loved the law, or he had never died: I only loved myself. The honour of his Father's law was dear to him. Heb.* i. 9. *Psal.* xl. 8. *Matth. v.* 17, 18. *Myself alone was dear to me. I viewed his death, his dying love, as all for me. His agony in the garden, his bloody sweat, his dying groans, all out of love to me! This pleased my heart.—His Father's glory I had never seen: The law's beauty I had never beheld: The wisdom of God, in the death of his Son, I had never brought into the account.—Love, love! love to me, to me! was all in all: This only ravished my heart. I loved myself, I only loved myself.—Strange, that I should think my love to Christ so great! The very joy I had, to think he died for me, was a full proof that I loved him not at all; since I did not delight in the law, nor love the law, in honour to which he died. Had my wife or child, or friend, or any whom I loved, been punished by that law, I had been full of grief, and thought it very hard: For indeed that law appeared to me like the laws of Draco. But when* CHRIST *was the victim, I was pleased:*

Oh! my dear Aspasio—in the time of the late rebellion, when I lived in England, had I, through a hearty attachment to the Pretender's interest, secretly poisoned ten of the house of Lords, and twenty of the house of Commons, from mere spite, only because of their loyalty to their rightful sovereign; and had I laid a plot to blow up King and Parliament, burn the city of London, and deliver the nation into the hands of a Popish Pretender—all through pure malignity, what would it have availed before a court of justice, after I was arraigned, convicted and condemned, to have pleaded, "Oh, spare my life—I am sorry for what I have done—I will never do so any more—I will be a good and loyal subject for the time to come!" Especially, if all the court knew I was a jacobite by blood, and had shewn myself a jacobite, in ten thousand instances, all my life long, and had still very much of the heart of a jacobite; and had lived and died a perfect jacobite in heart and practice, were it not for some irresistible arguments, or rather something more powerful than arguments, that had begun to give me a new turn of mind? Would my penitence be esteemed any atonement for my horrid crimes? Nay, rather, would not the whole nation cry, "Away with such a vile wretch from the Earth, for he is not fit to live!" And were I brought to view the whole affair in a right light, and to feel right; what would be the language of my heart? Would it not echo back the general cry? "Right! right! away with such a vile wretch from the Earth! for, indeed, I am not fit to live!"—And on the gallows, even in my dying agonies, I should not have the least reason to dislike the law, by which I was condemned; or to love my judges ever the less, for pronouncing the sentence of condemnation upon me. But rather, with all my heart, I ought to approve the law, as good; and esteem their conduct to be truly praise-worthy.

But to murder thirty of my fellow-worms, blow up King and Parliament, burn a city, ruin a nation, viewed only as

For I loved myself: but CHRIST *I did not love. I cared not what he suffered, nor why; if I myself was safe. In truth, if the law is not* holy, just and good, *glorious and amiable, the death of* CHRIST, *to answer its demands, is the most shocking affair that ever happened. But I was wholly swallowed up in self: And,* " *if I was but safe, I cared not how.*"

injuries to a civil community, and breaches of a civil law, are no crimes, in comparison with rising in rebellion against the INFINITELY GLORIOUS MONARCH OF THE UNIVERSE; compared with whom, the whole created system is *less than nothing and vanity*.(1)

Wherefore, in my best frames, in my devoutest hours, when I feel the greatest veneration for the Deity, and the greatest regard to his law, and am most sorry that I ever have been, and am still such a vile rebel against my rightful sovereign, the GOD of GLORY; I am so far from thinking that I am fit to live, that my whole heart is ready to say, "No—but infinitely unfit to live! Eternal death is my due! And Hell my proper home!" Yea, it appears to me, although I had attained to love God and Christ in the same degree as Saint Paul did, and were as willing to die in the cause of Religion as he was, that yet I should merit Hell every moment for not loving God and Christ more. And therefore, with him, I would *have no confidence in the flesh*; and would seek to be found, not in myself, but in Christ; not having my own righteousness, but his. Phil. iii. 3. 9. And would say, *In the Lord* alone *have I Righteousness, and in him* alone *will I glory*. Isai. xlv. 24, 25.

Yea, suffer me to say, I apprehend and verily believe, that even Saint Paul himself deserved eternal damnation, for that wickedness which God saw in his heart, then, at that instant, when a little before he died a martyr, he said,

(1) *Is it a Sinner's duty to be willing to be damned?*—NO, *by no means.*—*The damned will forever hate God: The Sinner ought forever to love him. The damned will be forever miserable: The Sinner is invited to be forever happy, through Christ. His duty is, to be reconciled to God, and return to him through Jesus Christ. Indeed, were there no other way to support the honour of the divine government, but by the eternal misery of the Sinner, the Sinner ought to be willing, that the honour of the divine government should be supported, although at the expence of his eternal sufferings.*—*God and Christ, Angels and Saints, will all be of this mind, at the day of Judgment, with respect to the wicked. And they will all judge rightly. Rom. ii. 2.*—*Nor will the wicked have any reason to dislike them for it; but, rather, to esteem their conduct herein truly praise-worthy. Rev. xix.* 1, 6.

I am now ready to be offered. For although he was willing, quite willing to die for his master; yet he did not love him perfectly as he ought. He himself owns, he had *not already attained, nor was already perfect*. But the least defect deserves punishment, yea, eternal damnation. Therefore, Saint Paul always felt in his heart, that Hell was his proper due; and always looked on the law, even as a *ministration of death and condemnation*, to be *glorious* (2 Cor. iii. 7, 9) and always placed all his dependance, for acceptance in the sight of God, on Jesus Christ. He did so, not only when first converted, but habitually, all the days of his life, to his very last breath.

O, in how lively, how striking a manner, are all these sentiments expressed in those words of the blessed Apostle, in Gal. ii. 19, 20; which were the genuine language of his heart, and give a picture of the inward temper of his soul. *I through the law, am dead to the law, that I might live to God. I am crucified with Christ: nevertheless I live; yet not I; but Christ liveth in me: And the life I live in the flesh,* even to my latest breath, *I live by the Faith of the Son of God, who loved me, and gave himself for me.*—*Who loved me*, as his own before the foundation of the world; and in the fulness of time, *gave himself for me*, as one whom the Father had given to him. For, in the midst of these holy views and gracious exercises of heart, Saint Paul's Calling and Election were always sure; and he steadily knew, that he was of that blessed number for whom Christ died, with an absolute design to save. Yet this knowledge was not the foundation, but rather the consequence of his Faith and holiness.

Your Theron does no more doubt of God's readiness to be reconciled to the Sinner, that returns to him through Jesus Christ, than he doubts of the truth of the Gospel. He believes the one just as firmly as he believes the other. If the chief facts related in the Gospel are true, he knows this consequence is equally true. If God has so pitied this apostate world, as to give his own Son to die a sacrifice for sin, to answer the demands of his law, and secure the honour of his government, for this very end, that *he might be just, and yet the justifier of him that believeth in Jesus*— and if he has testified his acceptance of the atonement, by raising him from the dead, and setting him at his own right hand in Heaven.—I say, if these facts are true, your

Theron knows the confequence cannot but be true, viz.—That any Sinner, how ill-deferving foever, who, upon the invitation of the Gofpel, fhall *repent and be converted,* fhall return to God through Jefus Chrift, he will be accepted, pardoned, and faved, for Chrift's fake. And, *beholding as in a glafs the glory of the Lord,* I cannot but return and give up myfelf to God through Jefus Chrift with all my heart. Pfal. cx. 3. Joh. xvii. 3, 8. Pfal. ix. 10.

Such were the views—fuch were the tempers of the Apoftle Paul, who wrote, and of the Chriftians to whom he directed his Epiftles; as he himfelf affirms. 2 Cor. iii. 18. And it was under fuch views, and in confequence of fuch tempers, that they were affured, the fpiritual and everlafting bleffings of the Gofpel were *theirs;* as another Apoftle afferts. 1 Joh. ii. 3, 4, 5. And in fuch views, and with fuch tempers, Saint Paul might well expect, that the confideration of the infinite goodnefs of God towards them, in their election, redemption, effectual calling, juftification, adoption, fanctification, and in the eternal joys of Heaven, to be certainly beftowed upon them, would powerfully animate them to *prefent themfelves a living facrifice to God,* to be for ever entirely his. Rom. 12, 1.

The Saints at Rome, viewed *the wrath of God as revealed from Heaven againft all ungodlinefs,* againft the leaft fin, felt themfelves *without excufe,* their mouths ftopt, guilty before God, according to law; a law holy, juft, and good— were therefore dead to the law and married to Chrift, exercifed Faith in the blood of Chrift, depending entirely on *free Grace through t e redemption which is in Chrift Jefus.* And as by virtue of their union with Adam, they became Sinners; fo by virtue of their union with Chrift, by a true and living Faith, they became righteous. And were *dead to fin,* fo that they *could not any longer live therein.* For they not only approved the law as holy, juft and good, but even *delighted in the law of God after the inward man,* and maintained a conftant conflict againft every contrary bias. For they were made partakers of the divine nature—had every one of them the fpirit of Chrift dwelling in them; and *walked not after the flefh, but after the fpirit*—were daily led by the fpirit, and lived under the government of divine grace, feeling the temper of children towards God; crying, *Abba, Father.* And if children, they knew they were heirs of God, and joint heirs with Jefus Chrift. And as they were willing to suffer with Christ, they expected to reign with him. And they esteemed the sufferings of this present life not worthy to be compared with the glory they had in view, in a future state. Besides, they found by experience, that all their sufferings worked together for their good, brought them nearer to God, and made them more like him. And they were persuaded that nothing in life or death should ever separate them from the love of God: who of his mere sovereign grace, had predestinated, called, and done all things for them; not because they had any claim to make, but because *he would have mercy on whom he would have mercy*; of the same lump, making one a vessel to honour, and another a vessel to dishonour. Which sovereign right to dispose of his own grace, they saw belonged to God; *of whom, and by whom, and to whom are all things; to whom be glory for ever!*—Wherefore, as the fittest and happiest thing in the world, they brought themselves, soul and body, as the Jew used to bring his bullock to the altar, and presented themselves *a living sacrifice to God*; seeking daily to be more and more transformed into the divine image, and devoting themselves, in all humility and love, to the duties of their several places—*not slothful in business, but fervent in spirit, serving the Lord.*—(Please to read the 12 first chapters of the Epistle to the Romans.)

The Saints at Ephesus also, who formerly had their *understandings darkened*, their *hearts blind* and *alienated from God*; yea, who were quite *dead in sin*; and so far from any right to claim mercy, that they were *without Christ, having no hope, and without God in the world*; yea, even *by nature children of wrath*: yet these, of God's mere sovereign grace, according to his purpose before the foundation of the world, were quickened, had divine life communicated to them, were *raised from the dead*, were brought to know Jesus Christ, and trust in him; in consequence of which, they were sealed, had the holy spirit given to dwell in them, whereby they were furnished to all good works. And conscious to this divine change, and to the glorious blessings they were now made partakers of, they were fervently engaged to walk worthy of the vocation, wherewith they were called—to live up to their holy religion—to forgive others as God had forgiven them, and in all things to imitate their heavenly Father, being followers

all with singleness of heart, as unto the Lord, &c.—[Please to read over the whole Epistle.]

But time once was, O my dear Aspasio, when your Theron, not conscious of any sanctifying operations in his own breast, believed all the blessings of the Gospel to be his—without any " evidence from Scripture, sense, or reason:" Which belief served to still his conscience, and keep him at ease, while blind to the beauty of the divine Nature, and a stranger to the divine life. And in this case, having no sufficient evidence from inherent graces, to support his confidence, he was obliged, without any evidence at all from any quarter, resolutely to maintain his belief, by believing. Oh, what awful delusion! How was I like one blindfold; one destitute of any sense or reason, or knowledge of the Scriptures, *led captive by Satan at his will!*—by Satan *transformed into an Angel of Light.*

Oh, my dear Aspasio, pity an ignorant benighted world, who love to flatter themselves, and to hear no cry from their teachers, but PEACE, PEACE :—And guard them against the sad delusion, which had well-nigh proved the ruin of your own Theron.

If all your sentiments, as they exist in your own mind, are exactly right; if you had not the least design to convey one of those mistaken notions, which your Theron imbibed from your persuasive lips; if he misunderstood just every word, and framed a mere chimera in his own head, a chimera you abhor with all your heart: Yet, O my kind, my tender-hearted, my dear Aspasio, pity an ignorant world, who are like generally to understand you as I have done; and in compassion to immortal souls, be entreated, once more to take your fine, your entertaining, charming pen, which commands the attention of thousands, and ten thousands through all the British dominions, in Europe and America, and warn poor Sinners of their dreadful danger; lest multitudes perish in the road—the bewitching, the enchanting road—once trodden by your own pupil; and to which, but for the sovereign grace of God, he had been forever lost!—It is the humble and earnest request of

YOUR EVER AFFECTIONATE

THERON.

END OF LETTERS & DIALOGUES.

www.ingramcontent.com/pod-product-compliance
Lightning Source LLC
Chambersburg PA
CBHW022134160426
43197CB00009B/1287